PURE
COACHING

A PRACTICAL GUIDE TO BECOMING
A GREAT LEADER

JAN RUDGE & HAYLEY GUEST

ILLUSTRATIONS BY DAN SMITH

PURE Coaching

Copyright © Jan Rudge and Hayley Guest 2021

ISBN 978-1-913713-25-6

Published by Compass-Publishing 2021

Edited and designed by The Book Refinery Ltd
www.thebookrefinery.com

A catalogue copy of this book is available from the British Library.

Dedications

Jan: To my parents Edna and Stan Rudge for giving me the opportunities which they did not have and for always valuing education.

Hayley: To Julie and Roger, the most wonderful mom and dad that a little girl could wish for!

A butterfly is a
transformation,
not a better caterpillar.

CONTENTS

PART TWO
HAYLEY'S STORY – 81

PART THREE
WHAT IS PURE COACHING? – 139

PART FOUR
MY LEADERSHIP LIBRARY OF INSPIRATION:
20 BOOKS THAT HAVE GUIDED MY LEADERSHIP JOURNEY – 185

Introduction

'The time is always right to do what's right'
Words to Lead By: Ken Blanchard

Welcome!

We are Jan and Hayley, a former and a serving head teacher, now coach and coachee. We are at very different stages in our careers in education, but both of us are on a journey that has overlapped.

We are writing from our school perspective, but with the conscious understanding that leadership spans many different businesses and organisations, together with self-leadership, getting yourself from A to B.

Our stories are about leading ourselves and others. We hope that you will find some thought-provoking and practical ideas to take into your own situations – ideas to help you reflect and move forward, not simply with hope that you will get where you want to be, albeit with an expectancy of stress, fatigue, fear and pressure, but with more empowering thoughts, leading to enhanced well-being, and providing you with energy, motivation and choice.

For some of you, having a coach may not yet be possible, so we hope this book serves as your guide and leads you to reflective thinking as you take action and navigate your own journey ahead.

We have two very different stories of how you get to headship and beyond. Whatever era you are leading in, there is one commonality: the need to grow the hearts and minds of your people; all staff, children, their families and other stakeholders. Both Hayley and I have discovered, as we worked together as coach and coachee, that our common belief in **growing hearts and minds** is synonymous with the progress and well-being of schools.

Creating a thinking space for a busy person/leader to have a period of reflection, reduces stress and enhances their mental health. This is not research based, but built on powerful testimonies of others who have been on the coaching journey with us. We think this is significant and

Stuff can weigh you down.
PURE coaching provides
a safe space to de-clutter.

so have chosen to share our stories and some of theirs, together with our chronological journeys, in the hope that you will find within our stories snippets of learning to add to your own career timeline.

So why PURE coaching? It is with a feeling of dismay that we acknowledge that much attributed to the concept of coaching in schools is about *performance.*

As with sports coaching, this is many people's understanding of the word coaching. On our journey we have come across leaders fearful of coaching, because their interpretation is that you have coaching when you are not good enough.

PURE coaching is PUREly your agenda and nothing to do with your performance (unless you choose to focus on this!). PURE coaching is developmental. By having a regular coaching time when you can stop and reflect on any subject that is taking up your head space, you feel 'lighter' and more 'empowered', helping you to bring your best self into your life.

You get back a feeling of control over your actions; you are less likely to get swallowed up by other 'stuff' and guess what: this leads to less stress and greater proactivity.

In Hayley's words: 'My coaching sessions keep me sane.'

Sanity. We could all do with a bit of that!

How to read *PURE Coaching*

PURE Coaching is non-directive coaching that is PUREly YOUR agenda.

Of course, you can start at the beginning of this book and read your way through it, but if you want to get straight into the how and the why of PURE Coaching, you may wish to start at Part 3.

Parts 1 and 2 contain reflective questions at the end of each section; if you like to journal, we hope that these questions will enable you to reflect on where you are at this point in your journey and what got you there.

If you are looking for further recommended leadership reads, Part 4 is a small reference library to dip in and out of, plus a collection of 12 top tips for you to keep in mind.

On the Pure Coaching website we share some agencies and sources of support, because coaching sometimes reveals that a person's needs lie beyond the expertise of the coach.

Whichever way you choose to read this book, we hope it helps to guide you forward and become the leader (or person) you aspire to be. Enjoy the stories we share while reflecting on your own life story.

PART ONE

JAN'S STORY

Introducing me, Jan Rudge

I love learning about leadership and coaching and I especially enjoy learning from others' experiences and from their stories. My leadership guru of 20+ years is Ken Blanchard; he has always delivered his messages through stories, many of which have become very memorable to me.

In this book, we want to open up a conversation about coaching in schools and why we feel the time is now right for a new non-directive coaching model, one that values both people and results; a system where people are partnered in their learning, not just led.

As my frustrations with the quality of school-centred coach training grew, taking action became a matter of *now or never.*

I met Hayley in her early days as an emergent school leader. She became a head teacher in 2012 and I coached her through this first headship.

In mid-autumn term 2015, there was a game changer as Hayley took her second headship of a three-form primary school. In January 2016, Hayley called Ofsted to inspect her 'good, if not outstanding school!' (even though the judgement was 'Requires Improvement' on the last inspection), Ofsted came and the (unsurprising) Special Measures journey began.

As a coaching advocate, Hayley continued to use her monthly coaching sessions to unpick and recreate East Park Primary in Wolverhampton; you will learn more about this in her story.

As the school went through its transformation, a system of training coaches, starting with the Senior Leadership Team and then middle leaders, with built-in supervision and ongoing learning began. A coaching culture emerged that became significant in the process of rebuilding this broken school.

Based on the East Park model, in 2018 I co-founded **Leadership Edge: Coaching in Schools**, specifically created to help other schools have a sustainable and affordable coaching culture in their schools.

This book will share my story, Hayley's story and the three-tier coaching model that emerged, together with the books and models I have found helpful, and the stories others have shared with us.

My aim for this book is to show how non-directive coaching – **PURE Coaching** as we call it – works in practice. The stories shared in this book are not solely about coaching, but about the core business in schools of leadership and pupil achievement through great teaching and learning. They are offered with the full understanding that what we share, and our experiences, are equally applicable to other organisations and individuals.

As a leader you have to ask
yourself the question:

At this moment in time,
what matters most?

1.

It's All About The Learning

I believe in *synchronicity*: things happening when they should. You meet new people, become inspired by something you read or listen to at that exact moment when you are receptive to the message. And, of course, bad stuff happens too.

My work lives include teacher, head teacher, leading a small Education Action Zone and working for the National College of Teaching and Leadership (NCTL), then starting up my own company, Leadership Partners. More recently in 2018, I started up Leadership Edge.

My home life continues its journey of change as a daughter to a mum with mental health challenges, who, in her 70s, became a self-published poet. I'm a mum to a wonderful son and daughter, and I continue to experience the joys of being a nan to my two amazing grandsons – and our shared love of ice cream!

Following two divorces, I stumbled upon my wonderful partner of now seven years, Steve. And I'm so grateful to my five special girlfriends who have stuck by me over the years, through thick and thin. All these relationships have brought their own rewards and at times challenges.

This is my journey, shared in the hope and expectation that somewhere within it, something will strike a chord with you, the reader, and you can add the learning to your own timeline.

Way back when...

I had a summer holiday job at a local hospital, where I sat alongside a trainee teacher who had just completed her first year of her teacher training. Over the course of our six weeks of working with each other, I decided that I would like to teach.

'Come to Loughborough,' my companion said.

So that's what I did!

How did I become a head teacher? Good question!

Although I share my journey to unexpected headship later in this section, headship was not my goal in my early career. I wanted to be a great teacher who made a difference. But, opportunities came along and I had the choice to take them or walk away.

Role models both good and not so good crossed my path, each experience signposting ways for me to further develop.

From class teacher, to middle leader, and year group leader in a four form entry primary school, I made the move to take up deputy headship in a one form entry primary school, five minutes up the road and a million miles away in its context.

The key questions anyone seeking headship should ask of themselves: where does your heart lie?
What does your gut tell you?

To say I disliked the early days of my deputy headship at Brierley Hill Primary would be an understatement.

As a deputy, you will probably spend more time with your head teacher than with your family. When making this move, *go with your gut reaction; ignore it at your peril.*

My relationship with my head did not serve either of us as both of us might have hoped it would. It was a testing time!

Fate intervened and the rest is history, as I subsequently (and unintentionally) became the head of Brierley Hill Primary. Here was a school where I could make a difference to children, many of whom had erratic home backgrounds, and the challenges poured in as a result.

I remember longing to talk to people about education and learning, but in truth I was the onsite social worker. With my deputy spending 50% of her time in class and the rest trouble-shooting challenges and fulfilling the SENCo role, it was nothing short of a miracle that our staff retention rate was high, with a team committed to serving our children educationally, emotionally and practically. And our children were making year on year gains in standards against the odds!

Prior learning only took me so far; again, fate intervened. My daughter, aged 16, was working in a local shopping centre. She was one half of *Snapper the Dragon*, the crèche mascot. It was hot wearing the costume and walking the malls, so she talked her way into Customer Services. She was invited to team training with Paul McGee (now known as The SUMO Guy after his book, *S.U.M.O. (Shut Up, Move On)*. She approached Paul at the end of a training session:

'My mum does your sort of stuff at her school up the road. You should go and visit her. This is her number...'

Subsequently, Paul visited me at school. He invited me to a speakers' group in Birmingham; this led to my attendance at a local speakers' group. It was my first time there when I struck up a conversation with the person sitting next to me.

'I'm going to find out about becoming a coach on Saturday,' she told me. We got talking. 'Come with me,' she invited.

I attended; she didn't. And I just KNEW, despite the hefty cost, that I needed to do this training. So I did, paying the coaching course fees in monthly instalments. The coach training (DipHE) spanned nine months. It was full-on (part-time!), comprising learning, skills training and coaching practice.

However, the WHY question kept popping up.

Why make *more* work, *more* studying, *more* learning and practice?

The answer came:

There is no point in being a head teacher unless you are a lead learner and have a strong moral purpose to serve your school and its community.

My time at Brierley Hill Primary from 1993 to 2002 was a roller coaster of emotions. I never doubted that I was serving in the right place.

It was new learning that moved me from the Brierley Hill headship to a fresh opportunity to lead the start-up of a small Education Action Zone in neighbouring Sandwell local education authority. My plan was clear: it was a two-year contract and then I would seek a second headship. It became five years in total. Fate took me on a different pathway.

Your future plans do not always work out as you think they will!

So, enter coaching; new learning, new thinking, a new group of people to learn alongside, all outside of education – and time to reflect; yes, this could indeed be useful in the day job and also beyond it.

In 2005, the term *coaching* was before its time in terms of the language used in education. It was to be a further five years before it began to be put forward as a possible strategy.

2007: I know I am now in the wrong job. I have a coaching session. My coach asks: **'How much longer before you take action?'** I take action and resign. The same week I get a call from NCTL (National College of Teaching and Leadership) following an email I had responded to months earlier.

Linking back to my opening comment and my belief in synchronicity and doors opening, this was a door I just HAD to walk through!

I am offered a three-days-a-week contract. As I sit in the car post interview, I get a call from a former head teacher colleague, who asks, 'What are you up to these days?' She is leading the Training and Development Agency in the West Midlands. 'Come and work for our team two days a week,' she offers. My working week is sorted!

As a coach, at the end of each section in Part 1, I will pose questions to aid your further reflections.

What are YOUR synchronistic moments?

- What were the defining moments?
- Who were the messengers along your way?
- What door did you choose to walk through?
- Which doors did you decide not to enter?
- Can you see a pattern forming?
- What 'messengers' might have passed you by?
- What decisions are you making right now?
- Is it plan-do-review or reflect and respond?

A great leader is a talent-spotter.

They know what you are capable
of before you do.

They also have a safety net to catch you
if you fall.

2.

My Journey Into Unintended Headship

Let me be clear – I am not a high-flyer. I've always been average at a lot of things and slightly better or worse at others. I remember sitting in a staff meeting at a large primary school as a youngish teacher, just listening to opinions being offered around the room. I was silent, and by the time I had thought what to say, someone else had said it!

I have been blessed to work for two wonderful head teachers, who were significant to my learning; they were also very different from each other, but both have added to my leadership repertoire. I have worked for other school leaders, too, who provided me with a different perspective on leadership.

As a new teacher in a one form entry primary, led by head teacher, Pete Welch, I learnt:

- The importance of clarity of message
- The importance for everyone in the team to contribute
- The importance of developing a common school language of learning.

Sadly, Pete got cancer and died aged 39. What a waste for the educational profession. You just have to learn from people when they are in your life.

Head teacher number two was Coral Johnson; what an amazing lady. Wise and formidable (I'm not sure that she would use these words to describe herself!), she grew the school from 84 pupils to 840! I went there on supply, then became a part-timer and eventually phase leader. The school in my era was a constant building site, well managed and expertly led. The amazing thing about Mrs J (I never could call her Coral, even when I became a head myself; I think it's a respect thing) was that she always knew what I was capable of before I did. She was a great talent-spotter and she also had a big safety net. I was to benefit from both.

As a full-time teacher, the time was right to apply for my first leadership role. I approached Mrs J tentatively to inform her I would like to apply for a Scale A role (very old leadership currency).

'Why?' she asked.

My first thought was that *I'd blown it! I am not worthy!*

'You need to apply for the B post,' I was told.

'I can't,' I replied. 'That's X's job.'

'Says who?' she responded!

I did as guided, applied and was successful.

My greatest learning from Mrs J was **the importance of talent-spotting and nurturing new talent with training, opportunities and feedback.**

She was quite simply brilliant at that. She also had a great sense of humour. In such a large primary, she was always round and about; truly visible.

I would go to Mrs J with a request and often get the response: 'I wondered how long it would take you to ask...' And I have endeavoured to build on what I learnt from her in my own leadership positions. My leadership toolbox was beginning to take shape.

My next step was when I attended an Aspiring Primary Deputy weekend course. I loved it and gained a huge amount of very useful information, including going through the process of applying for a deputy head position and then having a mock interview.

My letter of application was torn to shreds, in a very supportive manner! It was then reconstructed into a model or methodology that I still offer to others to this day.

Great leaders nurture
new talent with training,
opportunities and
thinking space to learn
from their own experiences.

It was to be a further nine months before a post came up that felt right for me to apply for. I was unsuccessful but, in the course of the interview process, met and bonded with the successful candidate, Tracy Ruddle, who was to be a significant colleague as we both moved into eventual headship and beyond.

I got the next job I applied for; it was a teaching role (most were in those days). I did, however, get one half day for deputy head duties. No PPA (planning, preparation and assessment) in those days either! I was responsible for collating attendance figures and the weekly diary; no mention of teaching and learning. It was great preparation for headship.

In addition to this, I was teaching a mixed Reception/Year 1 class, for which I wasn't a good fit. (In my prior role, I had been a KS2 coordinator.) Still, good experience, I told myself.

As educational leaders we are in the learning business. A leader has to contribute to teaching and learning at all levels in their organisation, whatever their job description states.

Thank heavens for a wonderful friend who was a 'born and bred' reception teacher. We adopted the 'you teach me and I'll teach the children' model. My learning was literally step by step. Like all teaching, if you love the job and love the children, then you go all out to give of your best to them. We all survived.

I went back to Mrs J at one point. 'I've made a big mistake,' I told her. 'Can I come "home"?'

She gave me a metaphorical kick up the backside. 'Go and do the job you have been appointed to do,' she said, then added, 'What can I do to help you?'

She was a great example of servant leadership.

A good leader asks: 'What can I do to help you?'

Fast forward a term and I found myself, now in Year 4, as acting head, as my head teacher was off ill. The term I have heard used is 'unintended headship'!

I had to learn fast. Thank heavens again for a wonderful business manager, who skilfully guided me through what I needed to do to keep my head above water. I was also blessed with very supportive governors.

The head returned. We sadly didn't enjoy the best of relationships; we just weren't aligned in our values or our thinking (be careful who you appoint to these key roles!). However, what I did know was that my responsibility was to be supportive. And I did my best.

Be careful who you appoint to key roles.
Is the person a good values and strengths match?

After four terms as deputy, I applied for my first headship. I was told I had no chance as I didn't have the experience but I applied anyway. I was shortlisted and got to the final two.

The school was a village school, not the urban primary in a challenging context that I was currently serving in. I felt, however, that I would not have been a good fit there and, looking back, I don't think I would have been happy.

The key moment in the final interview came with the question: 'Where do you see yourself in three years' time?' My heart answered loud and clear, 'Not here!' I can't remember what I said, but it wasn't that.

The right candidate got the role.

I returned to my deputy post to confirm that, indeed, I hadn't got the job, as the head had predicted.

However, fate played its hand again and the head was offered a part-time advisory role that then became permanent. The head teacher role at my school was now vacant, and I believed I knew what needed to be done to take the school to its next level of greatness. I applied and was successful. How did the quiet teacher who didn't speak up in staff meetings find herself here?

So, what would my present self say to my younger self about new opportunities presenting themselves? Ensure you have regular sessions with a coach to explore what is important to do and help you chart your course. Make sure you value and protect your time for these sessions.

When applying for a
leadership position,
listen to both your head
and your heart.

If one of them shouts,
'No!' – listen and act
accordingly.

All senior leaders and especially head teachers, CEOs and directors need a safe thinking space.

Charting your school journey: how has your journey in schools played out?

- Who have you learnt from on your school journey? Lessons may be both positive and negative.
- What will you seek to do as a leader yourself?
- What will you endeavour never to do?
- What are your non-negotiables and your why, as a leader or co-worker?
- Who are the people who joined you at significant moments on your journey? What was their contribution to your thinking and learning?
- What, in your eyes, does collaboration look like?
- Looking ahead, who would you value collaborating with?

It takes very little for people to feel valued.

3.

Life At Brierley Hill Primary

A rollercoaster ride!

Looking back over my time leading at Brierley Hill Primary, it's hard to remember the educational achievements, which there were. Instead it's the craziness that stands out, the stories that are shared when, with former colleagues, we glance back over this period of time.

Brierley Hill had its first Ofsted inspection in June 1999, a few months after the sudden passing of my beloved dad and my husband's departure to pastures new. The inspector, Martin, a serving head from Devon, arrived for his pre-visit looking a little bemused.

'I was expecting rolling hills,' he shared with me. He got high-rise flats, low-level council housing and a socially deprived community where the two big employers, Marsh and Baxter Butchers and Round Oak Steel Works, had both met their demise, leaving the town depleted of jobs, which had led to third-generation unemployment.

The local community around school was parochial; the nearest big town was Dudley, but it wasn't a place any of the children really visited. For them, life was Brierley Hill High Street. The new employer was the huge Merry Hill Shopping Centre, which opened in 1984. However, this wasn't a place the stalwart Brierley Hill folk would patronise: too exclusive and expensive!

A small, but not insignificant, employer was Wheeler Tubes, the steel stockholder over the road across the zebra crossing. It was encased with a tall steel fence. School was on the other side of the main road, hidden behind an old brick wall with cheap wire mesh on top of it.

It's fair to say, school wasn't in an affluent area. Inside, it wasn't the same, though; the current head had worked hard to make it bright and cheerful. The school logo was the briar rose. I mention this because I asked when I was first in post why the school logo was a pansy!

My number one BIG job as head: get the exterior wall and tatty mesh fencing down and let the children see out and people see in. The soap opera began. When I speak with new heads about their 'to do' wish list, I tell them about this project because it was a seven-year journey to transform the school's exterior.

In headship, you learn lots of things you were never previously even aware of.

There were building regulations, Highways Acts, health and safety executive meetings and council-led meetings to attend (again, sadly, I did not spend as much time as I wanted to on children's education!). By the year 2000, we'd broken through to the outside world, with posh railings, which were powder-coated in the newly termed colour of 'Brierley Hill blue'. I still feel pride in this perimeter fencing as I drive past today.

I always understood the place a school serves in its community. Families before the current generation had attended the school. We had history. I guess the need to *really listen* to what the community was saying was my first step into this coaching skill.

School was a scary place for many of our parents; staff were seen as 'different'.

Breaking down the barriers became an integral part of my Brierley Hill journey. Questions varied, from the easy ones – 'I'm in labour, what should I do?' My reply: 'We'll ring for an ambulance and arrange childcare' – to the more complex: 'I'm worried that my child will be snatched by my estranged partner' – not so easy. This became what was commonly known as a 'Tin Hat' job, which meant it needed to be a team effort.

I had to be creative. As I gained confidence in my role and stopped having unrealistic expectations (of talking education a lot), I recognised that life at Brierley Hill had to be about team: the staff (and certainly not just the teaching staff) became paramount.

The contribution of staff is paramount.
People need to feel heard.

At least twice a year, I had one-to-one conversations with ALL staff members – yes, even cleaners and lunchtime supervisors. I needed their support and contribution. I got it in bucketloads.

Looking back, I know I did this by simply following my intuition. A key question I would ask is:

How can we senior leaders best support you?

Questions also explored family lives, aspirations and dreams, and I shared my own. I remember being shocked to find out that my lunchtime staff liked children. You would never have got that impression by looking out of the window at lunchtime!

On the other hand, these staff had never had a day's training; they had never been listened to. They were surprised that not only did I meet with them each half term, but they were paid to stay on after their lunch duty and were given tea and biscuits.

The other wonderful group of people were our cleaners. They would gather at the end of the day in what was a decent-sized broom cupboard, otherwise known as the caretaker's stockroom. This was a great place to escape to if I didn't want to be found and I always got a warm welcome. As I would say to the ladies, 'This is the only time I can stop to smell the polish!'

I was constantly surprised that, despite the day-to-day challenges, of which there were many, staff recruitment was not hard and staff retention was high. People didn't leave unless for a promotion we couldn't provide. I would tell new teachers, 'If you can teach here, you can teach anywhere.' The support we provided for each other was over and above.

We had fun too. Our annual shows were legendary. They were written by a couple of talented teachers, often making the most of our pupils' innate talents and personalities. We always played to a packed audience. Staff were willing to dress up and be silly, and created wonderful memories. This won us a place in the heart of our community. It was clear we loved our children.

A teaching assistant taught us to tap dance and, as a staff group, we performed in the millennium 'Through the Decades' show. It was nerve-wracking but our efforts were appreciated by the audiences. This was a special time. I knew as staff we couldn't go it alone; we needed the help of the community, not just to come in and complain, but to feel and be part of us. The shows helped to create this unity.

Bring in the troops

I took to the streets, visited shops and local community centres. I actively recruited governors. At one point I had three vicars on our governing body. One of them, Tony, was also a member of the Magic Circle; great assemblies (tick – sorted!) and the joy of the children greeting Tony as he walked across the playground, finding coins behind ears! My rationale was that a good measure of divine intervention and a little magic could be just what we needed.

I also knocked on the door of Wheeler Tubes, the company over the road. I met with the MD and asked for his help with an idea for a Year 6 English/ enterprise project. What began was a five-year partnership between us, which we refined year on year.

Post SATS, Year 6 would have a visit to the factory. This was followed by a visit to school from the head of HR, who came with job descriptions from which they had to select one to apply for.

What followed was a formal one-to-one interview in the boardroom with the MD and head of HR. We scoured charity shops and wardrobes for interview outfits, and spoke to the children about professional dress and conduct in an interview. The added bonus was that the company gave us a cheque for £1000 a year; school became their sponsored charity. It raised more than we could at a jumble sale!

Rita from Asda became another star; she was the formidable and wonderful community lead. It was a memorable day when Queen Rita arrived at school to lead our Golden Jubilee celebration in 2002. Dressed resplendently and with a mask of Her Majesty in place, she led the whole school on a walking tour of Brierley Hill, assisted by the local police, with many of our families and residents turning out to cheer us on. This was followed by a whole school party on the front playground. Many watched with joy through our beautiful new railings!

Including people can make a big difference.

So, from the challenge of a duck being brought in, which sat in my office manager's in-tray, and parents shouting at me, to angry and upset children, we did find time to do some great learning too; the children but also the staff.

I discovered the joys of reading leadership books, especially those not related to education. Ken Blanchard became my favourite (and still is). I had a noticeboard in the staffroom of 'Jan's good reads'. I changed this display each half term, buying several copies of each book and leaving them lying around for people to borrow.

As a leader, your staff become your class.

It took me seven years, but I gained my Master's degree, with my study being around empowering children to have an 'I Can' attitude.

As staff, we modelled this, from presenting a swimming award to a lunchtime supervisor, to the discovery that our special needs teacher played the oboe in an orchestra; there was a hushed silence as our children watched in awe when she played for us in assembly.

Our aim was simple: we wanted all who were part of Brierley Hill to be happy and successful. We entered three of the National Education Awards, winning runner-up in Primary Teacher of the Year and IT Teacher of the Year and, in 2001, we were the regional winner in Supporting Parents, making the National Final in London.

Don't procrastinate, innovate!

At the time, nationally, some felt the National Teaching Awards were divisive. Not at Brierley Hill; it was a chance to celebrate our wonderful staff and to have fun! We talked together about who to nominate and the evidence behind the nomination and then asked that person to be our representative. The prize money was used at the request of the winner. We had a couple of wonderful prize-money-funded, end-of-term 'do's, where every member of staff was invited, partners too!

As a serving head, taking time to stop, reflect and respond was not part of my work diet. Life was a rollercoaster, with only occasional stops to breathe in school holidays.

I remember being envious of Dudley Schools, who formed part of one of the original and larger Education Action Zones (why was a school like Brierley Hill not included?). Each school was funded to recruit a learning mentor. How I would have loved one of these for our children. I guess my style was not to procrastinate but to be innovative. The conversation with a nursery nurse who worked in our nursery had revealed her interest in supporting parents. With a full intake of children, I was able to afford to bring her out of nursery and give her the title of Parent Support Worker: her job description was to 'do what is needed'.

She fulfilled the role brilliantly and our 'intelligence' in school rocketed. She was the last off the playground each morning and the first there at the end of the day; she cooed over new babies, sympathised over bereavements and prison sentences and forged new community relationships. By listening to our parents, we were better placed to serve them.

She drank endless cups of tea, contacted and supported parents with social services and became an indispensable team member. Her teaching award was well deserved.

Having become interested in the new National College of School Leadership, I was able to take control and applied with five like-minded heads in Sandwell and Dudley to become a Network Learning Community.

We were successful in gaining three years of funding to support our collaborative learning. This was a fabulous time, providing extraordinary professional development for staff and children across our schools. We called our network 'Gung Ho' after the book by Ken Blanchard. Our aims mirrored the book: our work should be worthwhile, we needed to be in control of achieving our goals and we would cheer each other on!

It was during these crazy times that I came across the term life coach.

With my Master's achieved, it was on to the next challenge. I came across a free online course funded by Newcastle College and my coaching journey began.

Keep your eye on the goal so children can achieve the best they can. Don't forget that staff achievements matter too.

I look back on the Brierley Hill era with fondness, although much of the time, the pressure and emotional toll was great. I wish I could have had a coach back then.

In the words of a recent Leadership Edge coachee:

'Your coaching time is precious. You need it. It's your space.'

What are you learning from your leadership journey?

- When have the unexpected happenings in your life led to new opportunities?

- If you are a leader, how and when do you create time for yourself to breathe and to think, rather than do?

- If you are on a rollercoaster ride, how will you be proactive and take self-care?

4.

One Thing Leads To Another

As the head in a challenging urban school, it was crucial that I concentrate not only on our developing the core skills that the DfE held us to account for, but that our focus was also on developing life skills. My Year 6 teacher (and PSHE lead) attended some training. It was there that she met a speaker who inspired her. Enter Professor Michael Bernard from the San Diego University, USA. 'You need to meet him,' she said. Next time round I did just that.

His PSHE programme was called 'You Can Do It!' (YCDI). This felt like a missing piece of our school jigsaw. We signed up and started to deliver the programme; we changed our school language to match. We were what Ken Blanchard would call 'raving fans'.

The clarity of the language you use in school should match your beliefs.

Professor Bernard was speaking in Birmingham. I sent six staff members to hear from the man himself, a huge expenditure for a small one form entry primary. I expected them to come back enthused. They didn't!

I wrote to Professor Bernard and asked: 'When my staff are so enthusiastic

*Which door will you choose
to walk through?*

about delivering YCDI in school and we are seeing the difference it's making to our children, WHY did they come back uninspired?'

Subsequent conversations developed between us and led to us sharing a platform next time he spoke in the UK. He spoke about the programme and I made it real by talking about the impact of delivering it in our school. It was a good combination and my first venture into being a speaker.

> *Talking about the impact of what you are striving to do strengthens your resolve to move forward and be proactive.*

Michael subsequently visited our school and spoke with our children about their YCDI work and its impact on their thinking. That year, all our Year 6 children achieved well in their SATs, the best results ever for our school.

We kept in close contact with Michael as the year progressed. I shared stories of individual children and the impact of a different mindset that some of them had achieved, leading to their greater success in both academic progress and social skills.

It was at the end of this, our first full year of delivering the YCDI programme at Brierley Hill Primary, that we held our leavers' service in our local church. Unbeknown to the children, I had asked Michael Bernard to record a message to those in Year 6.

I played the message: the children looked upwards as if it were divine guidance! At one point, Michael said, 'Daniel, I have heard great things about you. Are you there, Daniel?'

Daniel, an autistic child, rose to his feet and with arms outstretched replied, 'I am here!'

It was one of those rare, magical moments that will be remembered for ever.

One random day, I was checking emails and called out to my office manager, 'How do you feel about me going to California for three weeks in October?' She popped her head round the door. 'I don't think I heard you right,' she replied.

The email asked for expressions of interest from heads to do a three-week exchange visit to the Solana Beach District in California on a Fulbright sponsored programme. There was funding for ten West Midlands leaders.

'Go for it,' she said.

Food for thought. I went home, spoke to my two teenage children and then to my Chair of Governors. I had their blessing and the go-ahead to apply.

The assumption I made was that I had no chance and that they would have so many leaders, so much better than I was, to select from. The reality was that all of us who applied just about made up the ten. I was in!

If a door appears, you don't have to shut it before taking a look at what's on the other side!

We met up a few times to plan our visit with Tony, our group lead, always including a meal at the Indian restaurant he part-owned!

In October 2001, weeks after the tragedy of 9/11, we set off. On the plane, I sat next to Angela; to this day we continue to share an enduring friendship.

Synchronicity remained alive and well. I discovered, to my amazement, that the University of California campus, where Professor Bernard worked, was within an hour's drive from the Solana Beach school district. I informed him of our visit.

Simultaneously, an Australian YCDI colleague was also in the region. Michael promptly set up a conference at the university and my USA programme was tweaked to enable me to attend and speak.

On arrival in San Diego, we were individually 'claimed' by our host leaders; we were to stay in their homes for the duration of our three-week visit. We would then spend time at our particular host's own school, together with having visits as a group to other schools and their teacher training facilities, not to mention the unforgettable social programme, wrapped around our learning.

Julie was my host, a head teacher in a very wealthy part of Solana Beach. Her biggest challenge was managing all the 4x4s that arrived at the school gate to drop off and collect children, driven by the employed nannies, of course! This was all new to me and I did voice that Brierley Hill was in a somewhat different context!

It was a fascinating time, seeing how children's school experiences can differ so much, but with the same intent of serving the children to become great learners in their own rights. That much we did have in common.

Take parental consultations; all done in school time and where each teacher had a wishing tree – a vase of twigs, hanging from which were labels with wishes on…

'Our class would like a new set of tables and chairs, a tape recorder (in those days!), a set of reading books, a playground volunteer etc.' That's an interesting one to take back to school, I mused with a smile.

So it was that on one particular day during my US visit in school, a delivery lorry arrived with a set of furniture. 'Oh, that'll be a parental donation,' said Julie. Nothing new there obviously! 'Some parents choose to buy a gold or platinum brick,' she added, pointing to a wall of bricks with inscriptions on of children's names. 'They make a donation (of a said amount) to the school fund.' Hmmm…

I did learn SO much to bring back to school and some things we did implement in the time that followed. We all learnt such a lot from spending quality time together.

You can learn so much by spending quality time sharing focused learning with other/different school leaders.

In one conversation, synchronicity struck again. I met Marge Hobbs, the vice-superintendent of the school district. We had much in common. As we talked, Marge shared that she was lead trainer with Stephen Covey, author of *The 7 Habits of Highly Successful People*. I had read this book and was really interested to learn more. We shared the leadership leaders we followed; I spoke about Ken Blanchard's work. What was bizarre was that so many of the thought leaders resided in California and interacted with each other.

When synchronicity moves, doors open. Back home, Tracy Ruddle, who I had originally met at a deputy head interview (we had kept in touch since that day), and I, with four other head teachers, had applied to the then newly formed NCTL to be one of their *Networked Learning Communities*. We were successful and with a budget of £50k for three years, we developed collaborative practices in our schools and learnt alongside other communities nationally, bringing our learning together at termly conferences.

The first step into leadership is self-leadership, to know yourself, your strengths and your values.

This funding enabled us to invite Marge Hobbs to the UK to deliver a three-day programme of the *7 Habits* to a group of 20+ heads and leaders. From this training, I constructed a programme of six half-term twilight sessions, which is still being delivered some 16 years later and is known as 'First Steps into Leadership'.

First Steps is different every year and it is equally powerful each time. It's the participants who, between them, deliver the training to each other, with an experienced facilitator being in each session to draw the learning together and link the habits as the year progresses.

The programme centres on self-leadership. First learn to lead yourself before leading others. I love revisiting this programme year on year; there is always new personal learning!

In June 2018, Marge, now retired, revisited the UK and I was able to share with her how hundreds of leaders have benefited from that training she delivered. Her teaching is still having impact in our schools; what a legacy.

It was through the YCDI programme that I eventually decided to leave Brierley Hill Primary and take up the position of director of a new DfE-funded Education Action Zone in Sandwell. Its scope had the YCDI programme at its heart and its plan had been created and led by one of our Network Learning Community head teachers, who had also attended the *7 Habits* training.

In my later learning, I began to realise that my learning followed the now well-known and recognised Sigmoid curve developed by E. M. Rogers in 1962.

I personally like coach/author Whitney Johnson's work around this, which she terms 'Disrupt Yourself'. By identifying how your strengths, experience and innovative ideas can address unmet needs – what you do well that isn't being done – you position yourself to dive in at the shallow end of the S-curve, where the potential for success is greatest.

How have your opportunities developed?

- What opportunities have unexpectedly come your way?
- What made you pursue such opportunities?
- Who have been the significant people who have enabled or indeed blocked you from such opportunities?
- What have you learnt from these people?
- What opportunities have you let pass you by? Why was this?
- Can you track your journey in terms of the double or triple S-curve? When did the disruption happen and why was that?

5.

Enter The Coach

So, I was now a qualified and certificated coach. The great thing about being a part of this coaching community was the ongoing learning, in the form of face-to-face gatherings on Saturday mornings each month. Each session, a member of the senior coaching team would present some learning to the group. We listened, we shared group thinking around this learning and then we had space to further reflect in a coaching pair. This was so uplifting. It was also strange to be surrounded by proactive people without an agenda!

Have you spent time at work with someone with no personal agenda and where the focus is PUREly upon you?

I became conscious of my personal values and the impact of these on my work; they needed to be aligned. Values elicitation was a significant piece of learning on my coach-training journey. I have now incorporated this learning into both Leadership Edge coaching and into leadership training on the Growing Heads programme.

As a leader, can you articulate your personal values?

I continue to be alert to coachees' values coming through in their coaching sessions and ensure that I raise their own awareness of the impact of these personal values on their day-to-day challenges and opportunities. Knowing your own values can clarify self-understanding of a complex situation.

My challenge now was how to bring coaching into the school sector.

At this point I was director of an eight-school learning partnership in Sandwell, known as an Educational Action Zone. This was government-funded, bringing additional support into deprived communities.

I had developed good, trusted relationships with the school heads; there was much in the EAZ that was of practical benefit to their schools. I shared my coaching journey with the head teachers and asked if anyone would let me practise my coaching skills with them. There was reluctance! Wasn't this a bit touchy-feely? Eventually one of the eight head teachers did agree.

However, she wouldn't agree to learn more about herself through using the Strengths Based Leadership analysis (see *Strengths Based Leadership* by Tom Rath).

Many leaders continue to be sceptical about spending time on seeking to understand themselves before seeking to understand others.

With coaching still not on the educational horizon for leaders, I turned my focus to an aspect of my role, which was to engage with parents, to enable them to become partners in their children's learning.

The challenge was that I did not work in a leafy suburb where education was high on the parental agenda. It was the opposite. As one parent said to me, 'Why should I come into school? This is my free time when you have 'em!'

From the 'You Can Do It' work of Professor Michael Bernard, I created the 'I Can!' programme, a group resource to enable parents or community groups to become more self-aware and to make informed and reflective choices in their lives.

The programme is based on a non-directive coaching model and has many aspects of cognitive psychology within it. What made 'I Can!' different from other published programmes was its simplicity; it was an A6 size pocketbook with a key question per page:

How many times do I say
"I can't" but mean "I want to"

What can I do about this?

Figure 1: An extract from the 'I Can!' book.

Parents from our school group gathered weekly over a term and selected from the book the next two topics we would discuss the following week. Some sessions were emotive as parents shared challenges and experiences with each other. I took the role of facilitator.

For some parents who had experienced traumas of many different kinds, there were difficult sessions and many tears were shed. But, as with all coaching, once trusting relationships were built, people opened up and gained or sought the support they needed to move forwards.

What should not be underestimated is the role food played in such sessions. It was in the informal eating times that conversation really started to flow and people opened up: *feed the body, feed the mind.* The added benefit was that these people were often the meal providers at home; they appreciated someone looking after them for a change. The food was an incentive to regularly attend.

The sessions were subsequently handed over to the Learning Mentors in each of our schools, who had all attended the Train the Trainer programme.

The belief prevailed that, if we could support the parent, then hopefully they would feel confident to support their children and give clear and consistent parenting messages.

It was in 2009 that my first coaching breakthrough came through my NCSL contacts, with the reinvention of the National Professional Qualification for Headship (NPQH) and the inclusion of seven one-to-one coaching sessions to support participants on this programme. Over the next three years, I was to coach 72 new leaders and learn much about the challenges and aspirations of aspiring heads in all phases of education.

Many of these aspirant leaders would talk about their coaching sessions as being like therapy. One lady, whose school was around the corner from my home, would come and visit me for her sessions. She would sit in my comfy chair and put her feet on my footstool. Years later and well into her headship, she looked back on these times with gratitude, but still didn't see a coaching space as a priority for her own well-being. Busyness so often takes over.

As a coach, you can't help but learn too.
I learnt much about the challenges and aspirations
of future heads.

My own experience of headship was that such thinking spaces were not given urgency or priority; that it was selfish or a waste of time to create a safe space to think. As *well-being* takes increasingly greater priority, and the mental health of both adults and children is causing concern, maybe one day this will change.

Schools are all about IMPACT. It isn't easy to quantify the evidence that coaching works. You can look at attendance and reasons for days away from work; retention and recruitment are another quantitative marker. Beyond this, it becomes more qualitative around stress/happiness levels and the impact of challenging a limiting self-belief, or maybe acting more in accordance with your own values.

Trust

The bedrock of teamwork is trusting relationships.

Leaders will often focus upon teamwork, but trust is crucial. It operates on a spectrum:

10..5...0
I will trust unless you break that trust...
to, you have to earn my trust.

The bedrock of teamwork is trusting relationships.

Building rapport and trust is essential to any great coaching relationship. We call it the initial 'cup of coffee' session, where we begin to get to know each other. Coach and coachee open up, as they choose to, and share personal information. This is both powerful and essential if the relationship is to be of value.

As a coachee is willing to open up and trust in the protocols that wrap around each coaching session – those of confidentiality, being non-judgemental and honesty – then there are great benefits to be experienced. These can be life-changing as the coachee gains new insights into their own situations, both at schools and in their personal life.

The main body of evidence we are collecting is in the words of people who have been on their own coaching journey with Leadership Edge: the word heard more than any other is 'empowerment'.

It's not rocket science. If you want to empower your staff, provide a safe thinking space for them to explore their own agenda.

How well do you know yourself? Who provides support for you?

- What are your top three to five values? Can you articulate how these dominate your thinking and actions?
- Are you proactive or do you spend too much time procrastinating?
- When is your mind in overwhelm and you need to sort out your thinking?
- Who do you turn to when you need to share your thinking and feelings?
- What do you feel you have in common with parents you come into contact with?

- Do you feel (or does your job description say) that you are a coach, but you have never had sustainable training, supervision or coaching yourself?

- Have you ever received a coaching session, one where the agenda is PUREly yours?

If you want to empower your staff, provide a safe thinking space for them to explore their own agenda.

6.

Just Say No!

In order to say YES to something, often it means saying NO to something else.

The importance of knowing yourself is fundamental in enabling you to make the right choices for yourself.

I have learnt that going with my gut is important. My head alone will not deliver the best results. I have to know my values and align my actions to these.

Any leader who spends time eliciting their values and aligning their practices with their values will, I believe, be far more likely to live engaged and productive lives, and will have an increased sense of well-being.

Values are personal and unique to each individual. We may use the same word but attach a different meaning to it than another person. With fairness as my top value (having strength-tested this!), if I perceive something as unfair, I will always have a strong emotional reaction to it. I call this 'pushing my big red button'.

By acknowledging this as a values-based challenge, there are times when I need to put MY value aside and focus on the value that another person holds. This means that, as a coach, I can emotionally detach and keep the focus on my coachee.

'I mean you no harm'
should be the mantra of
every leader.

One of the most common challenges raised in both NPQ delivery sessions and in coaching conversations is, 'How can I say no to a leader?' – especially if you want to be seen to be making a valuable contribution or you aspire to a leadership promotion.

A skill we cover in our Practitioner Coach tier is managing your own monkey. In headship, I encouraged staff to come and have an honest conversation about priorities, and often through this, we were able to unravel them in what I hope was a supportive and developmental way.

On reflection, much of my thinking has been influenced by leaders and authors who have taken the time to put their thinking into books, podcasts and blogs: an amalgam of their thoughts with my own reflections and experiences.

In Part 4 of this book, I share with you the learning that has had the most influence on me. In your story, your list will be different. I offer this to you, as I will often ask others to recommend reading to me. Not everything will resonate but some may well.

For myself, I find that the key in learning to say NO is my own self-awareness.

- Knowing my personal values; what presses my *buttons* and why this is.

- Knowing my strengths and those of my team members: am I best placed to do what is being asked of me? Is there someone else on the team more able than I am?

- Knowing whether I align to my organisation's mission and values. Are these explicit? Talked about all the time?

- Knowing my life centre and the BIG PICTURE I seek to live by (Stephen Covey: *The 7 Habits of Highly Effective People*, Habit 2).

Saying NO is easy when the YES becomes your guiding light.

- I am now more aware that I need to be my authentic self.

- I cannot do what I don't believe in.

Saying NO is easy when the YES becomes your guiding light.

- I need to be true to myself as a leader when I am facilitating the learning of others.

- I do not need to reinvent myself.

- I will learn from the milestones on my own pathway.

- I need to always act with good intent: 'I mean you no harm!' is how I often describe a trusting relationship.

- I need to trust and further develop the skills I have that have enabled me to reach this stage of my learning journey.

Post pandemic (2020), it's interesting, as so many people I speak with are reflecting on the gains of lockdown.

My friend: 'We have a family Zoom every Saturday night with a theme. This week it was "share your favourite painting". We would never have been together and had this conversation before lockdown. Then we only met up two to three times a year.'

A school leader: 'One of the joys has been spending more time with my children as I have been working less in the evening.'

Connections: 'I have been in greater contact with family and friends as we have supported each other through good and not so good days. People have seen the need and rationalise time to do this! My Whats App groups have been busy. We've shared baking wonders, flowers in bloom, family stories, and what children's works of art our family youngsters have been creating, among many other things. It's uplifting.'

I walked more, discovered more places locally, spoke to more neighbours, clapped the NHS on a Thursday. I was more 'others' aware.

At Leadership Edge, we speak about the future of life in school as being *Adaptive Practices*; we need to be adaptable and responsive.

If we are to gain from the tsunami of the Coronavirus pandemic, will it be to respectfully and mindfully say NO in order to say YES to what matters most?

What have been your stand-out yes/no moments?

- At what times have you said yes, knowing that another task to complete will tip you into a stressful situation?

- When you have said yes, when you know the right answer for you was to say no, what was the true cost?

- Have you ever asked to talk through the 'one more thing' you have been asked to do? Negotiated a win-win outcome?

- What have been your gains during lockdown? How will you seek to continue some of the practices you have enjoyed during this time?

- When you now look back at the Covid-19 pandemic, what do you need to remind yourself of?

- What will prompt you to say NO, because of a bigger YES?

In PURE coaching, we deal with the complexities of work and personal life. What I have learnt through my own life journey to date has sown the seeds for the urgency of the need to create safe and confidential thinking spaces for staff in schools; more so than ever if our leaders are to be at their most effective.

Let's pledge to learn from the lessons of 2020 and get our priorities right – for ourselves and for the schools we serve in and with.

7.

Regrets, I've Had A Few

My mum loved the Frank Sinatra song, *My Way*, requesting this as the song to be played at her funeral. We dutifully obliged.

Intermingled with the S-curves of life, invariably black holes or 'blips' will appear from time to time; some are deeper and blacker than others. This may take us off course for a while as we seek recovery.

Here, I want to share my experience of a personal black hole; one outside my work but impacting on me, the person. I liken it now to having two tools: a spade and a ladder.

What happens when someone begins to exercise manipulation and control over you?

For me, this was in a personal setting but I am only too aware that it can also happen in a professional setting.

How can a situation that began by looking so full of promise and hope develop into a hole, which, on reflection and with hindsight, you CHOSE to dig for yourself?

Subtle behavioural changes can be so gradual, one degree at a time, day by day each one a further step into the hole. Suddenly, one day you face the facts; you give voice to your feelings that indeed someone is exercising control over you and that you are no longer being your authentic self. 'How did I let this happen?' you ask yourself over and over. By this time you are at the bottom of the hole.

Sometimes, when you look back, the answer is obvious as you revisit feelings of frustration, cover-ups, embarrassment and duplicity. Such is the sublety, that the changes in your own or another's behaviours can go almost unnoticed. Yet often onlookers can see what you can't always see yourself.

'How can someone like me,' you ask yourself, 'who, on a good day, can make sound, rational and well-thought-out decisions, fall into this sort of hole?'

To help myself and hopefully others understand, I now liken it to a cup of tea: if, each day, you add two or three grains of sugar less to your tea, how long will it take for you to notice that a similar drink someone makes for you tastes sweeter?

If you have ever had a manipulative leader, line manager, co-worker, subordinate or partner, how do you get a ladder to climb back out of your hole?

In order to understand this further, I turned to Covey's *7 Habits*. Habit 1: Be Proactive.

Suddenly, even taking a fairy step was huge to me, but slowly self-belief started to reappear and I was able to rediscover myself. My friends and colleagues were a huge part of my recovery; they supported rather than judged me. They didn't need to judge me. I did that really well myself!

> ### Sometimes, it's not others who judge us; we judge ourselves and often harshly.

In my quest to build my understanding of manipulation, I came across a great book: *Who's Pulling Your Strings?* by Dr Harriet Braiker (McGraw-Hill, 2004). I reached for my highlighter pen...

In a work context, there will always be people who seem to come along to test you. This can cause paralysis, or your feelings may engage in their own tug-of-war. As humans, we have emotional responses to feeling threatened. It's scary how often we hear such deeply personal stories pour out in a coaching session. At times, such emotional reactions catch

Coaching is a safe space
to hold silence, to explore
the root of a feeling and to
make a decision to move
ahead with a new mindset
of optimism and hope.

people unawares; at other times, people choose to be brave and share these deep experiences, which may have stayed with them over many years and resurface from time to time.

I was fortunate in having a long-term coaching relationship with my coach when my personal trauma needed to be explored further. He supported me through my melée of emotional reactions to having made a personal error of judgement with a relationship, which was having a hugely detrimental impact on my life. I lost count of the number of coaching sessions I spent dealing with this over a period of months and beyond; the pledges of actions and accountability I made in order to gradually move forward and change course. It wasn't easy for my friends and family to watch this play out; my coach was the one person who was without agenda or emotion. His support was essential in enabling me to take back control and act in accordance with my deeply held values.

That's when a support network of family, trusted friends and colleagues really pays dividends. However, one word of caution here is that of emotional attachment or detachment. My coach was the only 'team' member emotionally detached and therefore unique in the contribution he made; to hold that safe thinking space for me to move forward. He helped me to mould the future I wanted to create, to feel strong and less vulnerable once again.

Every leader needs a network of trusted people around them. One should be your coach.

When I started to see my experience as a learning opportunity, it was much easier for me to rationalise. I further deepened my learning around neuroscience and signed up for the World Business and Executive Coaching Summit (WBECS) intensive learning on Conversational Intelligence, led by Judith E. Glaser.

Judith spoke about the impact that our choice and use of words can have on others and how neurologically this has an impact on our behaviour. She introduced me to some great visual models, one of which was the Conversational Dashboard and another was the Ladder of Conclusions. Judith used the ladder to illustrate how reactions, feelings, thoughts and beliefs all contribute to the conclusion we draw.

In attempting to understand why, at times, I have allowed myself to be subtly manipulated in ways that go against my values and integrity, the Ladder of Conclusions was a helpful model. This model can be found in Judith's book: see Recommended Read 16 in Part 4.

The dilemmas of a leader

With a variety of stakeholders to hold you to account, it is inevitable that a leader can sometimes feel the pressures of accountability and be in receipt of opinions that do not align with their own. With governors and board members being urged to offer challenge, at times this can go too far (and at times not far enough!).

Being able to articulate your thoughts and opinions is a key part of being a leader, yet when do we practise what we know may be a challenging conversation? Mostly this rehearsal is done in our own heads.

What we know from neuroscience is that it is a different chemical reaction when we approach a situation from a point of low trust rather than high trust.

A coach will help you to cut out the noise of well-intentioned supporters and gain clarity as to your way forward.

Empowerment comes from articulation; what Stephen Covey calls moving from the mental creation, thinking in your head, and towards the physical creation, saying what you are thinking aloud (Habit 2: *The 7 Habits of Highly Effective People*).

That is why a coaching conversation is empowering; we articulate our thinking – sometimes in a haphazard manner, but that doesn't matter. With the support of our coach, we will refine our view and gain clarity.

We can rehearse potentially difficult conversations with our coach in advance of having them with another person. We can feel well prepared and at times decide what *not* to say. I have coached many leaders who, having rehearsed and subsequently held a difficult conversation, reflect on the value of having clarity in their approach prior to the conversation taking place.

'Take life a day at a time.
If you can't manage that,
take an hour at a time.'
Jan's mum

An NPQH coachee was, that afternoon, going into his new school, where he would soon be taking up his first headship position. He based his coaching session around the staff meeting agenda for that afternoon. By the end of the session, he had radically amended the agenda and, post meeting, emailed me to say, 'Thank goodness I had that coaching session. It would have been disastrous to have gone into school with my original agenda!'

Getting back to lessons I have learnt along my way, can a person whose trust has been betrayed by someone trust (anyone) again?

For me, to forgive and to forget are two different things. I still choose to trust new colleagues, friends and associates, until that trust is broken. And it's important to be trustworthy in return.

For any reader who currently finds themselves in a dark place, I am sharing my mum's words. She lived through several periods of severe mental-health challenges: *'Take life a day at a time. If you can't manage that, take an hour at a time.'*

What have been your 'black hole' moments?

- Have you ever made decisions that were not aligned to your authentic self to remain popular or to gain favour?

- Have you ever made a decision that has challenged a personal value?

- What have been your most challenging of times, both at work and in your personal life?

- How did you get out of each black hole?

- Which strategies or colleagues supported you? What did they do?

- What did you learn from these times?

- How have you supported others when you see them in a black hole?

More, more, faster, faster: Is this really the message leaders should be promoting?

8.

The Most Common Wish

One of the greatest challenges articulated by school staff that I hear when facilitating leadership training is, 'If only I had more time…'

I point out that we all have the same number of hours in our day, so why is it that some people appear to have more time than others? And why are so many teachers choosing to leave the profession after only a few short years? These are crucial reflection points for leaders.

My mum often quoted a poem, which she called 'Riding on a Treadmill', but is actually called 'The Escape', written by Brian J. Sanford.

In the poem Brian writes:

'I'm riding on a treadmill,
like a hamster in a wheel.'

The poem talks about how you make your escape from this situation, as,

'It's really not much fun.'

As I speak to serving school leaders, they often echo these sentiments. Many teachers are leaving the profession after only a few years and many leaders seek early retirement.

Press pause to reflect, recharge
and re-energise.

Is it about planning your escape from teaching, or making a worthwhile contribution by serving our young people?

It's not *more, more, faster, faster*, it's about *less is often more*. Press pause and stop to think: 'What matters most?'

I once heard a story that really resonated with me and I have often retold it.

A head teacher started at her new school. It was a good school. It had a well-planned-out skills and context-based curriculum.

On a closer look at timetables, the head noticed that the whole of Key Stage 1 had art on Tuesday afternoons.

Teachers, she noted, dutifully planned their art lessons according to the school curriculum, but often it was a challenge since the resources required were also needed by other KS1 classes. In conversation, she mentioned this to the teachers and asked why it was so.

No one seemed to really know, until one of the more established staff members recalled a caretaker from the past, who had said it would be much easier for the cleaning team to just have one 'messy' day to clean up from, and so Tuesdays became the day! No one had questioned this for many years; it was just 'the way we do things round here'.

The head spoke to the current caretaker about this. 'I don't like Tuesdays,' he replied. 'Why the classes can't spread out their art times is a mystery to me, but who am I to comment?'

The head gathered the KS1 team together and asked how they felt about Tuesday afternoons: it wasn't working for anyone! The timetable was swiftly amended. Everybody was happy. It was a quick win.

Taking time out to think is necessary.
It is a core principle of PURE coaching.

How many serving heads and leaders reading this take this time for themselves?

How many make time at the end of each working week to jot down their reflections and learning from that week, and leave with a clearer head as a result of doing so?

David Peterson, former head of coaching at Google, sees this as a key requirement for self-reflective and proactive leaders, and at Leadership Edge, we incorporate his thinking in the first part of the Leadership Edge Master Coach programme.

Would fewer teachers leave the profession if we pressed pause more often and stopped to listen to the thoughts and beliefs of each person as an individual contributor?

With retention being a challenge in schools, how are you as a leader building in conversations with staff for the future well-being of your school? Or, don't you have time to do this? If we want our staff to stay with us on the journey, we must listen to their career or personal aspirations so that, as roles change in response to need, we can then endeavour to line up potential new leaders for future roles. This will not happen by chance, but through a carefully constructed CPD programme, individually tailored to meet a person's strengths, values and needs.

As Judith Glaser emphasised in her work on Conversational Intelligence,

'Everything happens through conversation.'

This is both a starting point and ongoing process. It can be hard work! Success depends on the extent to which a person aligns to the shared vision and how this is communicated.

When do you have deliberate conversations and really listen?

- How much value do you place on having conversations regularly with your staff? Are you a leader who values listening to others?
- Would your staff agree with you?
- Would fewer teachers leave the profession if they pressed pause more often?
- What constructive actions will you commit to taking?

9.

Enter System Leadership: A History Lesson

My time serving at NCSL overlapped considerably with the personal challenges I was experiencing. This period became a contrast of light and shade.

While personally things grew ever more challenging, system leadership and the wonderful bunch of colleagues I was working alongside became my light. I had a renewed sense of purpose and direction. Added to this in 2011 with the birth of my first grandson, I now had a very different source of joy and purpose.

As a head teacher, I had engaged with NCTL (then NCSL) from its early inception. Keen to learn from others outside my network, this became an environment for future and serving leaders to learn **'from, with and on behalf of each other'**.

Under the visionary leadership of (the now Sir) Steve Munby and his team, a wonderful learning environment was created, bringing people together who had a passion for shaping education to meet the future needs of our children. The ability of this organisation to bring together the most creative minds in education, both within and outside England, and to showcase different ways of working, meant it became a hive of talented leaders willingly sharing their experiences with those who were willing to be involved in its work.

Can you imagine having a job where your role is to find the best creative ideas in the region (West Midlands in my case) and enable the authors of those ideas to meet with others to share their journeys and experiences? What a joy!

The wider Regional Leadership teams were as diverse as ours and a wonderful mix of primary, secondary and special education leaders.

A new breed of National Leadership programmes emerged through NCTL, as the recognition that leaders make the difference became an undisputed fact.

The new NPQs created a three-tier programme for middle and senior leaders and prospective heads. Having the NPQH (National Professional Qualification for Headship) became mandatory in 2009.

Those years, from 2009 to 2012, I feel when looking back were good ones. NPQH delegates were provided with seven sessions, with a leadership coach to 'hold a thinking space' for them as part of their training entitlement.

From 8th February 2012, applicants were no longer required to hold the NPQH qualification before taking up a substantive headship. The cost of the coaching service became prohibitive and in 2012 coaching in the NPQH programme became an 'extra', which schools were asked to fund; unsurprisingly few did. Shame!

In 2017, the NPQs underwent another transformation, with content that was felt to be more relevant to the next generation of leaders. Out went community cohesion; in came risk and resource management.

Many serving head teachers comment that the qualification in its current form remains far from perfect, and doesn't really prepare newly appointed head teachers for the job they are required to do. But can it ever do this?

Schools are diverse communities where real challenges, beyond standards of achievement, are part of the unknowns of everyday life. Opportunities for collaboration with peers are there in some multi academy trusts and federations, but it is variable.

So, what will this mean for schools, governing bodies and those aspiring to be our future head teachers?

This process of system leadership was fulfilling the research within the four 'Think Pieces' created by David H. Hargreaves, looking at how schools can create a sustainable, self-improving school system. The first of these papers was published in 2010.

Hargreaves' research identified four areas where schools need to develop in order to work well with other schools:

- Making the most of the benefits of clusters of schools.

- Using a local solutions approach.

- Stimulating schools to work together.

- Expanding system leadership.

In 2011, NCTL were instrumental in introducing a new collaborative approach known as Teaching School Alliances (TSA); a collaborative venture to support schools beyond their own existing network and fill the gaps of the ever-dwindling Local Authority resources.

One hundred of the best schools were selected, using a point-scoring application process. Part of the criteria was that the school must be graded as Ofsted Outstanding.

This was not a money-making venture. Each TSA received £40k per year to deliver on what became known as the Big 6:

1. Initial Teacher Training

2. School-to-School Support

3. Succession Planning

4. Talent Spotting

5. CPD

6. Research and Development.

From the initial hundred TSAs, year on year more schools became designated across the country, at its height totalling over 800 TSAs. However, the 'set' criteria didn't always geographically make sense, and hot spots with a large number of designated Teaching Schools who ended up in competition with each other were in contrast to cold spots who were under served.

In 2012 came Hargreaves' next Think Piece on 'Leading a Self-Improving School System', which looked at how the self-improving school system had developed since 2010. This report concentrated on the roles and responsibilities of school leaders.

With the start-up of Teaching Schools, there was now the double challenge to:

- co-develop professional practice that raises standards across their alliance
- work with other teaching schools to develop new standards of professional practice.

In the third Think Piece in January 2012, Hargreaves looked at school-to-school partnerships in an international context, showing the importance of creating the right culture for partnerships when building a self-improving system.

In Think Piece 4 on 'Increasing Maturity' in October 2012, Hargreaves concentrated on the nature of deep partnerships between schools and the actions needed to achieve them.

Looking back and living through those times in my role at NCTL, what seemed in those days like a million miles away from where the system was, has slowly but surely become common practice. I was saddened to see the NCTL close in 2016.

In 2015, the DfE announced a new national role of National School Commissioner (Sir David Carter), with a supporting team of nine regional commissioners (RSCs).

What is the role of the RSC? The RSC had the power to allow schools to convert to academies, sending warning notices if academies performed below expectation, and deciding whether schools could expand or reduce their intake. Each Regional Lead created a head teacher advisory board to support their work, which also became a forum for setting up challenge boards in under-performing areas.

The years 2016 and 2017 saw the introduction of the first 22 Research Schools. Their collaborative work with the Education Endowment Foundation took one of the Teaching School aims and shaped a suite of teacher-friendly research reports, with the content and layout being both simple and informative to school staff.

The Chartered College of Teaching, with its focus on teaching not just leadership, took up its Charter in 2017.

Also in 2017, the SIFF (The Strategic School Improvement Fund) programme was introduced. Bids were made for funding to support local areas of need. Few were successful in gaining the bids and huge amounts of time were spent by leaders in putting such bids together. The first programmes began in autumn 2017. By summer 2018, this was terminated as the DfE prioritised the funding to be spent elsewhere!

In 2019, enter English hubs to match currently established Maths hubs (founded in 2014). Led by schools with an outstanding record of early-reading teaching, the aim was to support other schools to deliver excellent early language and reading teaching in Reception and Key Stage 1, including age-appropriate phonics and essential next steps in reading.

It had to be acknowledged that many TSAs were not cost effective or indeed effective! Hence the next change in 2019 was the announcement of the 'Test and Learn' pilot of teaching school hubs, bringing together TSAs and groups under a central structure.

As we enter a new decade:

Be assured that change will be constant.

New ideologies will come and go. The one constant is that our children still need to be educated, to be served by a generation of school leaders who have their eye on the horizon.

Where will these leaders come from?

Fingers crossed, it will be from those leaders who seek to serve and not be served. Current servant leaders, who recognise that they must listen to their people, recruit to values and train for skills, who are lead learners, who read to learn, and articulate their learning in forums where they can challenge thinking and have their thinking challenged, will develop the next generation of leaders.

Leaders who seek to understand that when they use a non-directive coaching style to support their team – not as a quick fix, not as a precursor

Children

Staff
leaders

Self

The servant leader: serving staff so they can serve our children.

to a support and challenge plan, but because that's the way we bring our best self to work – will both serve and empower their staff.

How will your recruitment process get you the best-fit staff member?

- What makes a good recruitment process?

- Do you recruit in the traditional way or have your tried something different?

- How do you build your team for a strengths' balance?

- Do you enable your staff to be the best they can be by encouraging their personal development?

- Think of times when you have listened to staff and implemented their suggestions. How did this inform your future thinking?

- Have you ever taken a risk with recruitment? How did this play out?

- What part was played by your gut reaction?

- Have you ever taken on two staff when advertising for one vacancy?

PART TWO

HAYLEY'S STORY

Introducing Hayley Guest

From my Learning Community days (2002 – 2006), I had coached an emergent, and subsequently a designated head teacher, Hayley Guest, through her first headship.

In mid-autumn term 2015, there was a game changer as Hayley took her second headship, this time of a 720-place primary school. In February 2016, just weeks after she'd taken up the post in January, Ofsted came and the (unsurprising) Special Measures journey began.

From the start, Hayley delivered on her belief:

'We have clever kids here!'

She would be heard saying this over and over as she walked the corridors of the 700-place school. Hayley was clear that the children at East Park deserved teachers who were passionate, committed and great classroom practitioners. Staff who didn't wish to be part of this new journey left and were replaced by those who saw the mission and wanted to be involved in it.

As a coaching advocate, Hayley continued to use her monthly coaching sessions to unpick and recreate East Park Academy in Wolverhampton.

In the first year, she set about recruiting the team that would help her to get from where they were to a place where children felt safe, secure and successful. The strapline became (and still is) 'Growing Hearts and Minds'. It ends each school assembly, a reminder to all of what their school stands for.

Low standards and low self-belief were gradually replaced by higher aspirations within a culture that recognised teamwork, co-operation and contribution, from adults and pupils alike. As the school went through its transformation, a coaching culture emerged that became significant in the process of rebuilding a broken school.

The key statistics term by term are shown within the East Park story. Pupil standards have risen and results have improved alongside staff CPD at all levels. Parents in the school community are wonderfully supported by the two Julies, both trained coaches who have begun to develop a parent coach programme.

As the school went through its transformation, a coaching culture emerged that became significant in the rebuilding process. Leadership programmes, in tandem with a holistic coaching culture, focussed on a non-directive approach.

The Leadership Edge three-tier coaching programme was created during the East Park journey, as staff were empowered to bring their best selves to school. Coaching is now the bedrock of school improvement.

> ### Coaching is not an add-on; it is inclusive; it's 'the way we do things round here'.

In June 2019, Ofsted returned. East Park Academy was outstanding in all areas and their results put them in the top 10% of UK schools nationally. East Park was formally recognised as an outstanding school with coaching at its heart. The East Park Academy strapline of 'Growing Hearts and Minds' was a reality.

In this section, Hayley Guest, Head Teacher and Leadership Edge Master Coach, will share her journey from her early days of childhood, through to taking East Park from Special Measures to Outstanding. She will also share with you the role of coaching in this journey.

This was Hayley's response to the DfE on hearing that East Park was named in the top 100 most improved schools in 2019:

'As a long-standing advocate of coaching, I began to develop a coaching approach that enabled leaders, in the first instance, to be the best that they could be.

The Strategic team began to coach each member of the senior leadership team, providing them with a safe, confidential thinking space where they could explore whatever they wanted to explore. We describe this as 'PURE coaching'. This could be directly associated with their leadership role but could also be used to tackle personal challenges too.

The impact of this was felt immediately as we began to see leaders lead! By exploring their ideas and strategies, through coaching, they were able

What's the ONE big thing?

to act independently and were empowered to follow through with their considered strategies.

The voice of East Park was incredibly important throughout our journey: the voice of the children, the staff and our families. It sounds obvious but we talk and listen to them all the time! By actively engaging with everyone and actively listening, we were able to shape our school using our whole community and our coaching approach started to spread!'

You can simply feel the energy when you walk into some schools.

East Park Academy is an amazing example of energy in practice, but what (as always) makes a difference is the quality of leadership, and the ongoing learning and personal development for each and every staff member. It has been my privilege to be Hayley's coach on this journey.

East Park Academy is the Leadership Edge flagship school and, each term, visitors are welcome to visit and see the school day in practice.

Throughout our coaching sessions and especially as the East Park journey has developed, there has always remained one question that's asked at the start of each session (essential when so much needs to happen swiftly!): What's the one BIG thing?

Having achieved Outstanding in September 2019, the school is now leading two other schools, new in their trust, who are at a development point in their journeys. Staff from East Park are seconded to support these two new schools; great professional development for all. Vibrancy, an overwhelming optimism, care and love for each other are what this school is all about.

10.

In The Beginning

I always wanted to be a head teacher, right from the age of five. I would watch my head teacher, and distinctly remember thinking at that young age, why didn't he talent spot?

My best teacher was Mrs Smith; she was incredible. She lived and breathed learning. She made sure even Wesley Cooper learned. No other person I met in our primary school journey together did this! She taught us things other people didn't think we needed to know. We learnt about osmosis and mitosis, which at the time was on the GCSE syllabus.

Great teachers capture children's interests and create a love of learning

This is what Mrs Smith did all the time. I remember thinking, 'Why isn't our school making more of her? Why isn't every class taught by Mrs Smith?'

When I was nine, I recall her going for a deputy headship. She didn't get it. As a child I was relieved! As an adult now, I think, what a waste. If she had the impact she did on all the hundreds of children she taught at my school, think what an impact she could have had on so many more as a leader.

Fast forward. I became a parent helper in a school. I have always loved the smell of packed lunches! I walked into Springfield Primary and could smell that smell again. I was halfway through my degree at the time. I then got the opportunity to become a parent governor. I was curious; I wanted to know more.

There was a new route into teaching: The Graduate Teacher Programme. I shouldn't have been on that programme. My degree was a 2.2, not the 2.1 needed to be eligible.

There was another twist to this tale: my degree was with the Open University and results were not out until November. The course started in September!

The then head teacher of Springfield asked me what was in the carrier bags I was holding. I told him I had written to all primary schools to see if they would have me on their GTP programme. I had written 90+ letters to all the primary schools in Sandwell and Dudley.

Springfield agreed to take me and work around the slight problem of no degree as yet!

Fast forward again. I gained my QTS at Springfield and started my NQT year in Year 3. My NQT year began with two training days, led by Jan and her co-facilitator, Tracy Ruddle.

It was a vision and values day to bring together the infant and junior staff in the amalgamated Springfield Primary School.

Here was I ready to inspire and conquer the world, but I found myself in and amongst a group of passive learners, apart from my now deputy, Janine Sargent, who was among this group.

Surely as teachers and leaders we should have an enthusiasm for learning.

Jan and Tracy introduced us to the book, *Gung Ho!*. This started me on a learning pathway reading other Ken Blanchard books, and recognising from this early stage that my leadership development would come from other places beyond education. Since those early days, business-related books have always been a source of inspiration as my career developed.

From here, I discovered the NCSL Fast Track programme. I took the same approach to getting on the GTP course: I pestered them. You needed a First Class Honours degree to get on to the programme. I kept pestering them and eventually I got a place on the assessment days.

No doesn't mean no!

Part of the assessment day was written work and then there was the role play. I remember someone mentioning at the time that this is what heads do as part of NPQH.

'Great,' I thought, 'this will be good practice!'

So here I was just out of my NQT year, a permanent contract in my hand, with both my children attending the same school, and I was accepted on to Fast Track.

A condition of Fast Track was that I either worked in a series of primary schools in quick succession to gain depth and breadth of experience, or I went to work in a school in challenging circumstances.

Enter Corngreaves Primary, where Tracy Ruddle was the head teacher, having taken on the school when it went into Special Measures the previous term.

I met Tracy very soon afterwards at the checkout of a local supermarket, and tapped her on the shoulder with a tube of gift wrap. 'Gung Ho, friend!' I said.

Little did I know of other conversations that had taken place about my potential prior to this, about how I would be a great fit at Corngreaves.

You don't always know what's happening behind the scenes.

Springfield were not impressed as my children and I all left! I have always stuck out like a sore thumb everywhere I've been. Convention is not my style.

My coaching journey started through the Fast Track process with Will Thomas, who himself wrote *Coaching Solutions* (Network Continuum Education, 2009), and some years later awarded East Park Academy Coach Mark Gold.

How are you being proactive in your career development?

- How intentional are you about your own career?
- How do you respond to being told no?
- How creative are you in your development and journey?
- What is your passion? Are you following it?

11.
The Corngreaves Years

I have always found myself in schools in socially deprived and ethnically diverse areas of the Black Country, in the West Midlands. Cradley Heath was once a thriving local town centre, known for chain-making in the past and its parochial approach; they look after their own. From the 1970s, it became increasingly ethnically diverse. Today, with out-of-town shopping centres, it is mainly charity shops, food outlets and Tesco dominating the landscape. The area has high unemployment often going back several generations. Folk in the Black Country tell it how it is: as is often said, Black Country people are not 'backwards in coming forwards'. I was a good match for this approach!

Tracy Ruddle, having offered me a teaching post, placed me in Year 2, and I spent the summer painting my classroom. On day 3 of being at Corngreaves, we had the phone call for the second HMI inspection, but my first one.

My Year 2 children were lovably wild. I had just managed to get Gaige Bennett off the drainpipe in the corner of our old Victorian classroom when our HMI inspector arrived to observe the lesson. I got a 'good'! This was the first specific feedback I had ever received.

The Corngreaves journey was symbolised by the importance Tracy gave to CPD. This was the way she raised standards across the school. I learnt the importance of the development of people in order for this to happen.

To rapidly raise standards, you have to develop your people.

Until then, I had never been part of this type of development and to this day I still use some of the learning from those times.

Synergy strikes again! Corngreaves was fortunate to be part of the EAZ, which, by this time, Jan was leading. Tracy and Jan worked closely together, often co-facilitating training as they had that day at Springfield.

At Corngreaves, I witnessed first-hand how Tracy gathered and shaped her leadership team. She had a deputy and appointed three new assistant heads in a one form entry primary.

Recruitment became known as 'Ruddle Recruitment'. This comprised of finding the right person for the job, talking to them about the opportunity and creating the recruitment path from there. Job descriptions and the HR process came later. It was strengths-based recruitment, driven to match the need.

All leaders at Corngreaves, with the exception of Tracy, taught at least 50% of the time, and the rest was spent driving rapid school improvement. This led us from Special Measures to Good in two years. A year after Corngreaves were inspected again, it was graded Outstanding.

In my time at Corngreaves, I learnt the essence, the nuts and bolts of good teaching. We stripped things back and took risks to gain rapid school improvement.

Corngreaves became one of the first hundred Teaching Schools in 2011. In the early days of Teaching School, I was one of the goldfish in the Corngreaves bowl. Hardly a day went past without visitors coming into our classroom to watch us teach and to share our practice. I became well versed in articulating my classroom practice and talking learning. Looking back, and with no disrespect to this part of the journey, learning was often rote at this time.

Quality teachers can articulate learning with clarity.

During my time at Corngreaves, I became special education needs co-ordinator (SENCo) and assistant head. I also achieved the National Professional Qualification for Headship (NPQH), completing my second placement at Manor Primary in Wolverhampton. I had a coach during this placement too, who provided seven one-to-one (what at Leadership Edge we call PURE coaching) sessions. My agenda was to use these sessions well to chart my course ahead.

Corngreaves was federated with another primary school close by, Timbertree Primary, which at this stage was also in Special Measures. My role changed and I became AHT across both schools. This was not an effective strategy so, the following year, I was placed as head of school at Timbertree.

At this point, Janine Sargent came to join me as AHT from Springfield; a relationship that has endured the test of time with many an interesting twist and turn.

What have been your moments of great learning?

- How aware are you of points of learning around you, whether you need them now or in the future?

- What have you learnt about the features of rapid (school) improvement?

- Have you taken a calculated risk? What did you need to consider?

- Do you search out opportunities, or wait for them to come to you?

12.

The Timbertree Era

Timbertree was also in Cradley Heath, although there were very small pockets of private housing and a park. As is traditional of Cradley Heath people, they were proud and often vocal. The ability to fluently speak in a Black Country dialect was to my advantage.

The same inspector I'd met at Corngreaves was leading the inspection at Timbertree. I now had the opportunity to work more closely with her on the strategic development and level of challenge I needed to rise and respond to.

As I became officially the head, for the first time I was able to take on my own professional development. Part of this was my commitment to the value coaching holds for a serving head. Jan became my coach and saw me through my Timbertree years and beyond.

I remember using my coaching to formulate and carry through a support staff restructure.

During this time, it became clear that, although I had always wanted headship, this was not the way I'd envisaged it! I had little say in any of the strategic decisions beyond the running of the school. The destiny of Timbertree was out of my hands and I had no influence.

I started to put into practice developing people in the way I believed in. I spotted talent, nurtured staff from temporary contracts to substantive ones; at the same time I was able to craft opportunities for people to move on into roles outside our school that were more suited to their strengths.

Good leaders spot talent, nurture it and create opportunities.

There is a value that should not be underestimated in the importance of heads having a wide network and being outward-facing. At this time, I was a serving governor at the local secondary school, which created development opportunities for our staff and theirs.

By 2013, with a divorce pending, I had a clearer vision for what I wanted headship to be.

A new era dawned. Challenges emerged with the academy chain over finances, which led to the lack of choice and connection I experienced. This was out of alignment with my growth in competence as a head, one of the three Cs (choice, connection and competence) that underpin the work of Susan Fowler.

Susan talks about suboptimal and optimal levels of motivation. At this point I was experiencing external motivation (suboptimal), and I identified through coaching that I was not in a position to flourish because things that mattered were out of my control.

In one of my coaching sessions, I remember saying to Jan, 'I need a new challenge!'

I needed this new challenge to be in a school that had a significant journey to go on; a school that would allow me to be the head teacher I wanted to be. I didn't want to be restricted in my professional development.

The search began. In the process, I spoke with Anita Cliff, CEO of Manor MAT, where I had previously spent time on my NPQH placement. It was through this connection that a new opportunity arose, which was a good match for my strengths and elicited my passion to go on a new school improvement journey and to make a significant difference.

The interview was interesting. I'm not sure how many three form entry schools appointing an experienced head teacher would insist that candidates teach as part of the interview. I was asked to teach in Year 3; incidentally, I was the only shortlisted candidate! Suffice to say, alarm bells began to ring. Interesting from this day was the SIP who quietly said to me, 'Know your worth.'

In subsequent learning, I have learnt that research shows men are much better at articulating their worth than women. Time for some girl power!

On that day in September 2015, I was appointed head teacher of East Park Primary.

The next part of my journey had begun.

Know your worth.

Are you bringing your best self to work?

- As a leader, do you know your worth?
- Who can you directly impact and make a difference to?
- Are you flourishing in your current position?
- How would you describe your current level of motivation?
- Do you recognise when you need a new challenge?

13.

The East Park Journey: Part 1

Autumn 2015 to July 2016

East Park is a 720-place three form entry primary school in inner city Wolverhampton. The key difference was the move from headship in a town to one in a multi-cultural, diverse city, with deeply rooted social challenges within the community.

At the time of my appointment, it was a school with the Ofsted judgement of Requires Improvement, from 2013. The infant and junior schools had been amalgamated in 2011.

My East Park journey started the week after my appointment, when board members at Timbertree agreed a secondment of two days a week during the autumn term, prior to my officially taking up post in January 2016.

The two days a week provided me with insight that was integral to the journey. Here are some of the highlights I discovered in those early days:

- Illegal safeguarding processes.
- Poor HR practice, with the appointment of staff who had no risk assessment for identified concerns from their DBS.

- Financial irregularities.

- A devalued and demotivated group of staff, who had been habitually abused over a significant period of time.

- Extreme behaviour at every level.

- Children significantly underachieving.

- A culture of fear, felt by children, staff and parents.

However, the one thing that was in place was a tea-towel policy. If you find yourself in need of a model policy, do feel free to use this one.

Do you need a tea-towel policy?

Jan remained my coach through this transition and to the current day. My coaching sessions became ever more important: what was I to tackle first? To have that thinking space was crucial at this time; it cleared my head and gave me a path forward.

> ### *Coaching cleared my head and I was able to create a path forward.*

What I also recognised very quickly was the need for a highly effective deputy head. There were currently ten leaders on the leadership pay spine and teaching was minimal among this group. The current deputy was the acting head; his whole teaching career had been at East Park, providing him with limited experience and leadership skills.

I used my first SLT session to identify roles and responsibilities from the perspective of each individual leader. What was clear was that they were not familiar with articulating their daily responsibilities and accountabilities.

The school had also appointed five NQTs who received minimal support in this first term. What I uncovered, too, was that the NQT reports required by the local authority were written by the NQTs themselves, and this had been the case for many years. This was a cause for concern!

I knew the ideal candidate for the DHT post. Janine came with me, and was appointed in October 2015. We both took up our substantive roles in January 2016.

My first meeting with governors in the autumn term was interesting. I took along the RAISE report.

'Oh, we don't use that!' they said.

'Unfortunately,' I responded, 'Ofsted do!'

One of the urgent needs at this point was coaching the governors to understand their responsibilities, and opening their eyes to the realities of their role.

I was learning about East Park rapidly during my two days a week. I felt by looking in the eyes of the staff that there was more to tell. I knew there was an urgent need to rapidly gather evidence of school culture, procedures alongside standards, and to get to know our children. This had to begin as soon as I took up post.

There was a rapid need to gather evidence.

I remember that coaching session well as I explored the ways to gather this information. I made the decision to send out an email to all staff, with three simple questions on it:

1. What was positive about the previous East Park culture?

2. What was negative about the previous East Park culture?

3. What would you like to take forward to the new East Park culture?

Within 24 hours, I'd had six emails back to ask if the information they were about to share was for my eyes only. I responded to assure them that the information they gave me (despite knowing the email address of the respondent) would be treated anonymously. Then the floodgates opened.

Without that coaching conversation, I wouldn't have been able to gather in the amount of information from these different perspectives. It gave me intelligence to work from and helped me to understand where these people were coming from.

The same process was then repeated with children using a Big Brother diary pod, which saw senior leaders interview each child to elicit their views. One question they were asked was:

Do you feel safe at school?

Their responses both verbally and visually were shocking and had many parallels to those of the staff. There was a lot of fear around.

A feature of our journey was that we kept talking to people and listening to their responses. It was important that we kept having these conversations. This went some way towards helping staff feel valued.

Communication was key; messages were repeated with clarity, often over and over again. Why did we do that? In the hope that they would hear!

Messages were repeated with clarity over and over again.

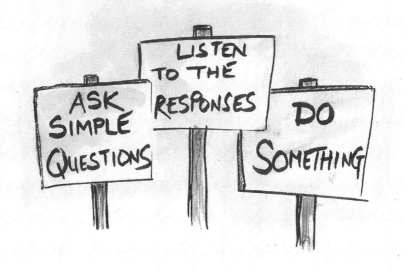

Ask simple questions.
Listen to the responses.
Do something!

However, communication did more than that. People started to recognise that the part they needed to play on this journey was important. Staff began to feel valued and heard, a key feature of what was later in the journey to become PURE coaching sessions.

The gathered information was used to create our first INSET day on 4th January 2016. I began with:

'You know your children far better than I do at this minute: what do you think the children said?'

Responses were over-inflated and no one reflected the children's reality. Our children, like the staff, were fearful.

On this first day, I announced to all staff that there was to be a restructure due to needing to show value for money. We approached everything at East Park with clarity at its heart. Nothing was a shock; staff had heard it before from me.

Weekly newsletters were started immediately. They would be sent on a Friday to staff and to parents on a Monday. This continued the consistency of message. Everyone in the organisation knew what we were doing and why we were doing it.

In the first few days, some significant SLT members decided that the road ahead was not for them and chose to move on. The process we had begun had helped them to see their future was not with us on this journey.

In order to get a clear picture of teaching and learning across the school, every member of staff was to be observed teaching, starting with myself and Janine. This exposed that good role models in teaching and learning among the former SLT did not exist.

Good teaching and learning role models are essential to achieve rapid improvement.

As this process rolled down from middle leaders to all teachers, it became apparent that the profile of teaching and learning was significantly weak. Our immediate priority turned to the support that East Park could not provide for its five NQTs.

I sat them down and explained that it was unlikely they would succeed in their NQT year due to the necessary support required that we were unable to provide for them. With support and collaboration, four were found new placements and one remained, who successfully completed her NQT year.

There was a real need for decisive leadership. The safeguarding complaints, along with many other warning signs, warranted an alert to Ofsted. I did this in many ways, by email, by post and by phone, and kept on until they duly arrived in February 2016. Our Special Measures journey had officially begun.

The local paper had been hounding me since the day I started, to defend accusations that had been brought to their attention. The only time I responded was post Ofsted, when I encouraged them to wait for the report.

When the report did finally appear in the press, I walked across to our neighbouring shops. One shopkeeper called me to one side to say that he had saved me the last copy. Good communications were flourishing; clarity was being seen, even within our community.

By the end of the first term, the vast majority of the SLT had moved on, along with a number of teaching staff, including the four NQTs.

I remember, one Monday morning, ringing Jan to inform her that six resignations had been pushed under my door. There were two in particular from teachers who had missed the spring term resignation date. To their surprise, I willingly accepted them. In fact, many comparisons at that time were made between the leadership office door and that of Harry Potter, when he also received special letters!

Summer term began and at this time, so did the first real conversations about coaching. We needed to find some way of developing leaders, who had little or no leadership development but maybe had potential, and making them effective and independent leaders as quickly as we could for the following September.

During this term, we also appointed two new senior leaders, who were to start with us in the new academic year. This was the making of our new strategic leadership team.

It's worth noting here that there was an interesting situation around one of these appointments. The school where the leader worked was itself struggling; assumptions were made by the local authority and there was a lack of judgement about the calibre of this candidate. Yet both myself and Janine had the most instinctive and positive reaction to this interview that we had ever had.

Always listen to your gut reaction.

We made the appointment and both regard this as our best appointment to date. This leader has been highly instrumental in the East Park journey.

In readiness for September 2016, year groups now had year group leaders for the first time, but they were inexperienced at this point. Time for coaching!

How do you go about sorting out your thinking?

- How do you currently clear your head?

- Who helps you to make sense of things? What do they do?

- In a new position, do you take the time to gather the information you need before shaping your vision?

- How well do you listen to those around you and to the messages you hear?

- How do you know that your messages are clear? What strategies do you use?

- How do you prioritise what needs to be done first, whilst looking after the well-being of yourself and others?

- How realistic are you about known challenges ahead? To what extent is it easier not to know?

14.
Decisions and the Box of Doom!

The challenge is that the more cupboards you look in and the more drawers you open, the more you will discover. I had a vision of what was possible, but the starting points and milestones kept on changing as I discovered new learning.

I include here some of the key decisions we made in those early days, all of which are factual.

I didn't have a magic wand; strangely, you don't get one supplied with headship. I needed to acknowledge early on that, being in an inner-city school, the levels of deprivation and pastoral need would mean that some issues would be longstanding. Schools do not go into Special Measures overnight; this was the result of way more than a decade of a poorly educated community and society around our school. The local secondary school had also been in Special Measures. To try to break this cycle was an enormous challenge.

It needed to be a long-term strategy; this was not just about our children but also their parents, who had made the transition from pupil to parent with a poor education themselves. In the words of Stephen Covey, we needed to 'seek first to understand, before being understood'.

I attended the staff Christmas 'do' prior to taking up post in January 2016. The staff were interesting too. I discovered internal personal relationships and a love triangle that was bubbling over into the school day. On calling the parties to speak with me, a slanging match arose, which resulted in HR intervention. Other male staff members had been in relationships with parents of our children. The community was holding on to past behaviours.

I was then in receipt of a steady flow of staff stories, from the crazy to the bizarre; the spectrum went from true to pure fiction! What was clear was that staff needed to get 'stuff' off their chests.

At staff meetings, staff would sit silently and wait for instructions. They didn't understand and didn't trust us when we asked for their opinions and ideas. They really didn't understand why Janine and I would spend so much time with them and the children. There was no comprehension of their importance in the process.

Decision 1: Janine and I needed to be visible.

We made the decision to be at the school gate every morning and after school. How parents engaged with our school through this journey would be crucial.

It was the same with our children; they were not used to seeing the head teacher around school. As I walked the corridors, there would be whispers of, 'Oh, there's the head teacher!' The same thing happened when I went into classes; there was a ripple effect. It took a while for this to be seen as normal. It told me a lot about the previous culture.

Decision 2: We needed to change parental perceptions of East Park.

It's true to say that many parents believed their children were at a good, if not outstanding school, when the truth was it had been a Special Measures school for some time.

Parents were very comfortable to come into school and stand swearing at the front office. One day I witnessed this and responded, 'Mr E, I can't possibly tell you to f*** off, so you can't expect to come into school and swear at us.' He started again. I had to forcibly tell him, 'Do not get angry in our school office!' The levels of observed bad behaviours were truly shocking and no one had been held to account for them in the past. It was just accepted as 'that's what happens round here'.

Decision 3: We needed a pastoral support team that supported!

There were two male support staff who were seen by parents as the staff able to restrain unruly pupils. Parents were shocked to be told that in school we would not be restraining their children!

In summer 2016, we appointed two ladies to be known as 'The Two Julies', for obvious reasons. Julie G had worked in both primary and secondary schools supporting vulnerable pupils; Julie W had been a member of a local authority Multi Agency Safeguarding Hub (MASH team). We needed lots of layers to our pastoral support.

Decision 4: We will have an open-door policy.

From the start, Janine and I decided that no one would be turned away from having a conversation with us at school. We needed to build trust and relationships with parents. This gave us unlimited opportunity to repeat, repeat, repeat the same messages. Previously parents did not see the head teacher unless an appointment was made, if at all! Lines of communication were poor and urgently needed to change.

Decision 5: Listen to the voices.

Each half term, we would send out mini questionnaires to parents, staff and children. We needed to hear their thoughts as we started our journey to better times. This gave us baseline qualitative information.

Decision 6: Communicate, communicate, communicate.

We established multiple lines of communication: every year group had an email address and contact number, along with those of senior leaders, the SENCo, the Two Julies and also my direct email.

I wrote newsletters to parents and staff each week, keeping them informed of feedback from pupil and parent voices. We took the risk and set up a Facebook group, which I managed. I responded to parents and was able to point out when their postings were inappropriate and take them down!

Decision 7: Be brave and encourage others to be brave too.

Have you ever had the joy of being faced by an aggressive/angry/frustrated parent? In this first year, Janine and I needed to inform Year 1 parents that their children would be having a fourth change of teacher that academic year. We didn't have time to see all parents individually, so we called a year group meeting. We were taken to task; they were baying for our blood.

We talked them round by simply being open and honest. We needed their children to have good teachers who would support their children's learning. I finished by saying: 'Am I going to come to you again about another change of teacher? Maybe!'

One parent who had seven children, three of whom were permanently excluded from secondary school, had her youngest child in Reception. The next child up fancied himself as a bit of a hairdresser and had cut his brother's hair and blamed it on someone at school. Mum turned up at the school gate with scissors in hand, shouting at me, 'I'll cut your f**king hair if you don't get to the bottom of who did this!'

I needed to take the risk that she might punch me. The police were called, and this resulted in riot vans and three police cars being sent to us! Another day at East Park.

It transpired from this incident that staff had also been in the firing line. Stories started to unfold. I couldn't believe that staff had become so accepting of bad behaviour from parents and children, that incidents were not reported. When challenged about this, staff response was, 'Well, these things happen in school, don't they?' Noooo!!

As our culture slowly began to change, so did our behaviour policy, which was adapted each half term to take account of where we were at.

The Box of Doom

One thing that is abundantly clear to me is the essential need for a leader to capture the journey from the beginning: enter the Box of Doom. During my induction days, I had started a collection of pupil books from every year group. It has provided a reminder of our starting point and is often referred back to. When I share this box with visitors, I suggest that they wash their hands after handling the contents!

It provides a comparison of the steps of progress made, term on term, year on year. It illustrates the expectations had and the impact made.

I needed to explicitly make children aware that their work would be for

My top tip for every leader in a challenging situation is to collate their own box of doom!

an audience larger than their class teacher's tick list. We started with a focus on presentation. This was to provide a quick win; it is something every child can be good at, even if the content leaves much to be desired. A child taking pride in their work was an essential step to increasing their personal drive and motivation. It provided a drip feed for children to achieve a genuine sense of belief in themselves.

What have been the key decisions you have made?

- How are you visible around school?
- Are you aware of parental perceptions?
- How do you manage the pastoral needs in schools?
- In what ways do you communicate? Are these ways effective?
- How brave are you? What brave steps have you taken?

15.

The East Park Journey: Part 2

Autumn 2016 to Summer 2018

My first full academic year at East Park saw the induction of our two new assistant heads. We had doubled our leadership capacity! Now there were four of us to tackle the challenges.

It was now common for parents to want to speak to me. This was becoming unsustainable, particularly on an hourly basis! With year group leaders now in post, we set up a new chain of communication, beginning with 'speak to the class teacher, then the year group leader before speaking to me'.

It was a personal challenge not to just impart a simple answer. To get the new communication system embedded, I kept redirecting them to the right person. The message soon sank in through this consistency of approach.

Be consistent in your messages.

Our new assistant heads were introduced to coaching skills across the autumn term 2016. This was followed by establishing coaching pairs between a year group leader and a senior leader.

Right from these early days I was asked, 'What should we use the coaching sessions for?'

'Whatever you feel is most important to you,' was my response.

This has been the mantra ever since! It's time for you to think!

From this point on, we never had to timetable or provide release time to support these coaching sessions to take place. Once people began to experience coaching sessions and to realise the impact they can have, this created optimal motivation.

At East Park at that time, there was so much going on that teachers and leaders needed this regular space to reflect on the next step forward and make decisions as to the actions they needed to take. Importantly, coaching sessions explored actions, so final decisions were well thought through. Coaching became the safety net; leaders felt a lot more confident because they had articulated various options before reaching their decisions.

An interesting challenge for me at this point was that, as much as Janine and I were on the same page with school improvement, Janine's prior beliefs about coaching made her cynical about the value and potential impact it would have at this stage in the journey. Nonetheless, as always, she was with me every step of the way.

The use of coaching throughout this year for leaders ensured rapid development for them, resulting in rapid development for the school. Despite this, the school standards, whilst improving, were still below national at all key assessment points.

January 2017: one year in and progress was being made in getting the right team together and making a stand on acceptable pupil (and staff) behaviour, together with the need for rapid improvement in standards – our children's right to a great education. This was so far removed from the inherited culture of January 2016.

By now we had moved from just me coaching, to three further strategic leaders having more coach training and experience. They are known to us now as Practitioner Coaches. The four of us continued to coach the other senior leaders during spring and summer term.

Further training and reflection revealed the need for people new to coaching to understand the coaching skills that their coach would be using, and to become familiar with the feeling of being coached.

We formulated non-negotiable protocols, confidentiality and being non-judgemental being the two crucial ones. We now call this the Foundation Stage.

During summer 2017, coachees quickly became confident in the knowledge that their sessions were purely their agenda, and their coaches became trusted in keeping strictly to the protocols.

Coachees were asked to complete reflections on their coaching journey and share these in a conversation – the early recognition of the importance given to articulating your own learning and stage of development.

This then led to the need for supervision of those leaders now in the role of coach, so we added a weekly agenda item to our SLT group to explore any common themes arising and challenges individual coaches might have experienced. Confidentialities were not breached.

Supervision led to the changing of coaching pairs mid-year. A regular feature of our supervision has been:

Do you feel that you are challenging their thinking?

As relationships developed, some coaches felt they were not offering the right level of challenge to the people they were coaching.

We changed coaches to ensure that challenge was always high and to avoid cosy relationships.

The East Park 8

We had school values and our strapline of 'Growing Hearts and Minds', but we needed more structure to embed values-based learning for our children. So we created the East Park 8 and, to date, these skills continue to drive personal and academic standards through the use of our weekly awarded stars in praise assembly. Children can get rewarded for their efforts in creativity, resilience, collaboration, honesty, respect, perseverance, self-belief and independence. In light of the recent pandemic and the changing needs in society, these have been reviewed and now reflect self-belief, independence, creativity, collaboration, with the introduction of kindness, responsibility and leadership, oracy and determination.

By summer 2017, standards were improving, but our children were still not achieving national standards. It became apparent that, despite having given our all to every member of staff who wanted to come with us on the journey, 18 months in, we knew that a small number of teachers still carried past baggage with them that was stopping them from becoming the teachers they and we wanted them to be.

We were at the end of the line and some challenging conversations needed to be held. These people subsequently moved on in their journeys.

At the same time, we were appointing new staff for September 2017, and we saw the biggest increase of 'new blood' into East Park.

The academic year 2017–2018 saw the biggest stride forward in the quality of education East Park was providing for our pupils, and subsequently the greatest rise in academic standards. By the end of the academic year, all national assessment points were in line with national outcomes. If you want to look at the data throughout the East Park journey, you will find this in the reference section.

In conversation with Jan during that year, we began to realise we had a structure that we were subconsciously working to: what we now call our three-tier approach, which is explained in the next part of this book. Our first Master Coaches were designated in summer 2018 and were to lead the ongoing coaching journey that, year on year, was expanding in numbers at East Park.

By summer 2018, we were in line with or above national levels at all key assessment points.

How are your school's vision and values shaping the actions you take?

- Do you have a vision? Have you tested out your vision? How might you do this?

- How do you influence others to buy into your vision?

- How do you manage your own expectations?

- When facing a knockback, how do you hold tight to the vision?

- Can you separate personal from professional rejection?

- How do you make recruitment meet your needs and help you to find the right person?

16.

The East Park Journey: Part 3

Autumn 2018 to July 2020

With new members of staff now part of the East Park team, I opened the opportunity up to the remaining 80 staff to express their interest in being coached.

We had a great response, with 27 staff volunteering, teaching staff, support staff, pastoral and admin teams. Some year group and senior leaders had by this stage progressed to the next stage of coaching – what is now termed 'Practitioner Level'. Further training had taken place and this group were now coaching and being coached themselves. Layers of supervision began to be developed. One of these was through a regular SLT agenda, but importantly, there were also individual opportunities to 'take the temperature' through regular, short, online questionnaires.

With more of the right people now involved, momentum was building. We had a good set of results; more staff had been in receipt of various CPD opportunities both within and beyond the MAT. This was an important year. Our systems, structures, our curriculum and appointment system were now our own: we now had a clear East Park identity.

Prior to autumn half term 2018, East Park was featured alongside Manor Primary and Hill Avenue Academy from our multi-academy trust in the Education Parliamentary Review. This led to a visit to parliament!

One Monday morning in autumn 2018, a random email popped through to the deputy head teacher's laptop, offering East Park the opportunity to complete the Well-Being Award. On reflection, this had been what our journey to date had been centred around.

She read the criteria and said out loud to me, 'We already do this.' Much of the well-being culture that had been established through PURE coaching meant that our staff were at the very centre of what we wanted to achieve.

This was exactly the same for our application to become a 'Coach Mark Gold' school. Both applications for the awards wrote themselves. Coaching had provided our culture with such a deep-rooted approach, impacting on everyone and everything, that it ensured our school was rapidly becoming a place where we were 'growing hearts and minds'.

By December 2018, both awards had been achieved.

In January 2019, the start of our third year, the inspection window opened.

The same levels of excitement were felt as the first time round, but for very different reasons. We were good to go as soon as the call came.

By now we were becoming known for being a school with a non-directive coaching culture, and where our children could talk about school improvement. More visitors were arriving and giving us the opportunity to share our development work, both in school improvement and coaching. We became the Leadership Edge flagship coaching school. For the first time, we had started to experiment with the process of junior coaches, enabling pupils to develop their coaching skills and support one another. These pupils were supported and supervised by one of our assistant heads, herself a Master Coach.

We waited and waited and waited... No call came until one day in June 2019, when we were informed that the team would be with us for the next two days. The lady who notified us of the inspection noted my excitement, and expressed that she would like to do the call again so that she could record it!

Here are my inspection highlights from our report:

- The quality of leadership at all levels is superb.
- It is an inspirational school and one that has much to share with others.
- Staff clearly value the support and challenge they receive.
- Leaders are unequivocal about the importance of staff well-being.
- Staff are vocal in their praise of the value and investment in their health and well-being.
- Many staff champion the way leaders have provided a work-life balance, giving them back a family life, while also improving their practice as a teacher or leader.
- There is a mutual deep respect between pupils and adults.
- Academic standards have risen significantly in the previous two years; these high standards are being maintained and strengthened further.

The two days were a dream. Our mantra of…

We challenge ourselves before anyone else does

… rang out loud and clear, and resulted in my giving the lead inspector a *high five* as the inspection officially closed and the team began to deliberate on the outcome!

It was official: East Park Academy was now outstanding across the board.

The following morning, a visit from a new Associate Coach with Leadership Edge was scheduled. Catherine duly arrived, but in the throes of post-inspection euphoria, found the strategic leadership team rehearsing their circus skills, spinning plates and juggling (in reality, not metaphorically)!

Some may argue we had been doing this for the two days before! But there was a reason for this behaviour. The year was to draw to a close with an amazing production of *The Greatest Showman*, hence the circus prompts!

It was a great tribute to our Year 6 children and the many staff involved; a show worthy of the West End.

In July 2019, SATs results came though, confirming what we already knew: East Park pupils had made remarkable gains in their learning. In mid-July, this was further confirmed with a letter from the Minister for Education, informing us that we were in the top hundred most improved schools in 2019!

The new academic year began with us receiving a letter from the Queen! Unknown to us, one of our Year 2 children, Faridah Gomina, had written to the Queen after inspection to tell her how proud she was to attend East Park Academy, and about the excellent reputation it had gained! She proudly brought the letter from the Queen into school. This was shortly followed by an invitation to The Queen's Royal Garden Party in summer 2020. Little did we know then what summer 2020 had in store!

The new school year, autumn 2019, also saw the beginning of spreading the coaching culture in and beyond our MAT. East Park now had a wealth of people who had been through the Leadership Edge accreditation process at all three levels. All of East Park's designated Specialist Leaders in Education were at least Practitioner-level coaches; a skill they were now able to draw upon as they went out to support other schools.

In addition, a further 20 schools in the Black Country had now taken part in the accreditation process and started their own coaching journeys. Many of these schools had been to visit us at East Park to hear the story of people's coaching journeys. The visits enabled others to see the results for themselves but more importantly to 'feel' the culture across school.

Undeniably a result of our coaching culture is the capacity of our leadership team at East Park – so much so that, from autumn 2019, our deputy head and one of our senior assistant heads were able to become acting heads of school in two schools within our MAT, pending new appointments of heads of school from January 2020.

In February 2020, the MAT hosted its first annual conference, with guest speakers, Jonathan Lear and Gavin Oattes providing us with a perfect balance between curriculum innovation and inspiration. Gavin's latest book had just been released, entitled, *Life Will See You Now* (Capstone, 2020).

Little did we know how this would play out from March 2020. The impending pandemic was getting ever closer to having an impact on school life as we knew it.

Schools were to close generally from 23rd March 2020. However, they would stay open for our key workers and our most vulnerable children.

Culture goes beyond a school's four walls; this period of time put this to the test. Established coaching pairs were encouraged to connect with their coaches and continue their coaching remotely.

From coaching at East Park always having been face to face, it seamlessly transitioned to remote coaching, using one of the online platforms available to us.

For some time, I had wanted to explore spreading coaching into our MAT family of schools. The pandemic gave me the opportunity to investigate further how this might work – through my coaching session, obviously!

I spoke to our CEO Anita Cliff and she fully endorsed this idea. I was happy to take the lead on this and began by contacting our heads and outlining the process and potential benefits it might bring. What the pandemic enabled staff to have was endless thinking time, but with a coach, they could refine their thinking and be proactive and future-focused.

At the start of the pandemic we had just East Park and Manor Primary with accredited coaches.

The plan was to coach across schools, using these accredited coaches, and hopefully involve staff from our other six MAT schools who had yet to become involved.

I sent an email out across all staff within our MAT, providing an introduction and theory session online. Twenty staff responded and took up the opportunity to start their own coaching journey. Stage one was to have a coach assigned and a virtual 'cup of coffee' meeting set up to get to know one another. This was then followed by two coaching sessions, then a theory session which explained and unpicked the techniques that their coach had been using with them.

Next, this group was given the opportunity to further develop by completing the Foundation Stage coaching accreditation with Leadership Edge. Of the 20 people, 13 took up this offer and have now completed this process and gained their accreditation (see more in Part 3).

The learning from this MAT-wide approach was that remote coaching, when wrapped around with a holistic system, created positive connections between the coach and the coachee, even though many pairs had never physically met at this point. It created an increased sense of curiosity, the perfect ingredient for a PURE coaching session.

As summer term 2020 drew to a memorable close, plans for our MAT professional development for the year ahead began. An email was sent to anyone involved in coaching to see if they would like to continue: there was 100% take-up. A further email to anyone not involved, to invite them onto the coaching journey, was sent. Over 100 staff across the MAT are now actively involved in PURE coaching!

How are you moving your organisation/school forward?

- What are your non-negotiables for personal and organisational success?
- How do you translate a successful initiative to include a more diverse group of people?
- How can you evaluate and measure the success of an initiative that is challenging to quantify?
- How do you take the temperature within your organisation?
- What new challenges have you taken on in the last six months?
- How do you drive your vision beyond your own circle? Do you have the opportunity to do this?

17.

Headships 1 and 2: Regrets, Repeats and Quick Wins

A significant shift happened between headship 1 and headship 2. Headship 1 happened *to* me: it was in many ways what Jan described as unintended headship. My first headship found me in the position, whilst I went looking intentionally for East Park.

I'm not really one for regrets; I don't see the point. However, I wish someone had pulled me to one side before my first headship to make me really consider the baggage that comes with becoming the head within your current school. When staff have known you as a fellow teacher and leader and then you become their head, it can bring with it its own set of challenges. Establishing myself as the head teacher of East Park was infinitely easier than trying to establish my Timbertree headship; much of this I feel was due to the previous roles I had held at Timbertree.

A regret for so many head teachers is not being fully aware about the headship they are walking into. Whilst I admit it's hard to know exactly what needs doing until you sit in the chair, the landscape for head teachers now is so much more complex. Knowing the political destination for your school is key, as is the school's financial position. This can have such an impact on its potential future.

Maybe I do have one slight regret: my immediate diagnosis of East Park. In the exuberance of my appointment, I remember saying to my deputy, 'It's just teaching and learning that need sorting.' My beloved grandad must have been looking down on me at that point as, thankfully, I ended up spending a significant period of time at East Park before I was officially in post – which allowed me to see that it was *sooo* much more than teaching and learning!

Top tip: never jump in with your solution before you fully know the school and how it ticks. This is crucial to enable you to create the right way forward. Thank you for the extra bit of patience, Grandad. We both know it doesn't come to me naturally!

Possibly my biggest regret during the East Park journey has been not looking after myself. Following my divorce, I had really invested in myself. I lost a significant amount of weight and was the healthiest and fittest of probably my adult life to date. After my appointment, I distinctly remember my deputy saying, 'No getting fat from Special Measures!' We both knew what was ahead for the school and for me. But I'm an 'all or nothing' type of gal; if you said my waistline was going to be impacted upon significantly as a result of the journey, I know I still wouldn't change a thing!

Being able to lead East Park Academy through its journey is and always will be one of the biggest achievements and honours of my career. Let's call it work in progress!

Every Special Measures journey is different. However, there are also elements that are exactly the same.

Developing people is fundamental. They make the difference to the children and families, as well as to each other. Constant investment is needed. This doesn't always require finance. Your networks are crucial to enable you to tap into expertise. The role of the Specialist Leader in Education has been beneficial for not only practitioners receiving the support but also the SLEs themselves.

In any challenging school, the priorities seem endless. You cannot address everything all at once. Identifying your one big thing is crucial, both in its identification and its communication. If I had remained with my thoughts that it was 'just teaching and learning' that needed sorting, we would still be in Measures now!

Self-care is very important – body and mind!

Quick wins

Establishing your relationships with staff seems such an obvious one, but actually getting to know them and how they tick takes much time and investment. However, every conversation and piece of communication is an investment well made. A school is the product of its culture and unless you get under the skin of it, you will only ever apply school improvement plasters.

So why have I put this in the 'quick wins' section if it clearly takes time? Because the impact of how you approach your staff with genuine inquisitiveness and curiosity can be felt *immediately* by them!

Challenging schools are full of speculation at all levels, from the staff, parents and even the children. 'How long are you stopping?' came from Joné (Johnny to most of us!) in Year 2 to my new KS1 AHT in September 2016. Suffice to say, she's still with us! Establishing clarity at all levels enables you to dispel many of the rumours.

Say it, say it and say it again

Say it at least seven times, the late, great Stephen Covey said. If you feel as though you are beginning to go mad with the same message, you may be getting somewhere near close.

What are the quick wins and the slow burns?

- What lessons have past experiences taught you?
- What does self-care look like to you?
- When it comes to quick wins, what has been successful for you?

18.

When Things Go Wrong

It may seem in reading the East Park story that all went swimmingly. Let me now dispel that myth!

For the sake of clarity, I will endeavour to identify what some of the challenges were and continue to be. As some issues get resolved, new challenges emerge.

Contributors to the journey

Any development journey, whilst having an end goal and vision, has phases to it. With this in mind and reflecting on the East Park journey, some people were destined to be with us for the whole journey and beyond, while some were only ever destined for a particular phase of it. The key to it is identifying the individuals correctly and trying to anticipate the next phase and who it will need.

I am thankful to everyone who created the East Park journey, whether they continue to be with us now, or were with us for a year, a term, or even less than half a term (yes, this last one actually happened!).

To take just one example, an experienced leader joined us early in the journey. School was in chaos; children had received on average two to three class teachers from September up to the end of the spring term due to early staff movement. This new leader was a ball of energy and had a genuine love of chaos! He enabled us to 'steady the ship', particularly for the class of children he was with. He was incredibly resilient and for that phase of the journey provided us with a model of resilience for the rest of the teaching staff.

However, he wasn't a long-term fit. As the chaos of school calmed, he began to create his own chaos. He was with us for just over a year and I was really grateful and appreciative for his input during this time.

Open and honest conversations

This was and continues to be the bedrock of our approach at East Park. It begins at interview. As already shared, we tend not to interview in the traditional way as we want to get under the skin of people to see how well they will fit the team. There have often been visits and many conversations before we get to the point of interview, along with a whole range of personality and team assessments, Patrick Lencioni's 'Humble, Hungry and Smart' assessment being a particular favourite of ours.

On a number of occasions, we found the right person for the team but they were applying for the wrong position at that time. This has happened frequently with potential leaders. Where many schools will often take the risk of appointing new leaders as the individuals demonstrate potential, we have had a very frank and open conversation with the individual along the lines of 'your skills and strengths really resonate and fit with our team. However, in the current phase of our journey you are not ready for this leadership position. If you are willing for us to work with you to provide the right training and experience you need to be able to hold this leadership position, we will commit to you beginning this leadership post after a year's worth of development'.

Each and every time this conversation has taken place, the individual has agreed, has taken the development opportunities and progressed in their leadership career. It tells you a lot about leaders when they embrace a development opportunity like that. They are definitely East Parkers!

Difficult conversations are supported by explicit training for all, not just leaders. In all roles, we need to have them, be it to challenge performance, to challenge behaviour or at times conduct. Having a skill set that supports these conversations is crucial, along with the opportunity to rehearse and practise. You won't be surprised to hear that our rehearsal takes places during our coaching sessions; an ideal place to explore and practise the delivery of a difficult conversation in a confidential and safe space.

People and their personal challenges

Challenging circumstances leave their mark on everyone in one way or another. As the journey started at East Park, we were working with a really damaged group of people. A large percentage had suffered workplace bullying and the vast majority were riddled with self-doubt and feelings of inadequacy. Simply insisting that people get better is not an effective leadership strategy!

At that time, we had a staff of over one hundred. A big part of the initial phase was getting to know them as individuals. Without that we would have had no idea how to make things better.

An influx of resignations has an impact on your staff group. Even the individuals you feel are strong and up for the journey can suffer from this influence. Taking the time to talk with every individual who made the decision to move on was incredibly important. As leaders, we need to evaluate the impact for both the individual and our staff.

For a small number, the emotion of the situation put them in a place where they actively sought out opportunities to have a negative input on our staff morale. This can be incredibly divisive. A resignation period of half a term can cause substantial damage. However, an increased awareness around this enabled us to limit this impact, which was essential for building the team through this period.

During the journey, there have been individuals who have flourished. One teacher, who had some of the poorest support and training in her NQT and RQT year, handed in her resignation from her teacher role and became a support member of staff for a period of time. This enabled her to build her confidence and self-belief. Within two terms she was back on her feet as a teacher and has gone from strength to strength. She is currently an integral member of our Year 6 teaching team.

On a number of occasions, we have appointed staff who brought with them significant baggage from previous schools and settings. Poor leadership can have a lasting effect on people, and unless this is unpicked

Never underestimate the influence of people's actions on others.

and addressed, that individual never truly moves forward. We have a duty to take care of the whole person. Ultimately, it is the whole person who comes to work every day.

One of these appointments affectionately labels East Park as the 'donkey sanctuary'. She assures me it is due to the fact that we put people back together and ensure they live their best life in the teaching profession, not that you come to East Park to be led out to pasture!

Hold tight to the vision when tested

Intensive school development is relentless. The twists and turns on the journey provide constant challenge. During our journey at East Park, we had to battle through other people's agendas; some wanted to have a positive impact and some actively wanted to have a negative impact.

Throughout all this, you need as many of you as possible to be holding tight to the vision. Clarity of this vision is essential. Unless we know what we want it to look like, how on earth will we ever get there?

This works alongside open and honest conversations and, where appropriate, directly addressing individuals whose agenda is not in line with us.

The Bear Hunt mentality!

In the words of Michael Rosen, 'We can't go over it. We can't go under it. Oh no! We've got to go through it!' (*We're Going on a Bear Hunt*, Walker Books, 1993). This is what we describe as the 'Bear Hunt' mentality. Throughout this whole journey, I knew what I wanted it to look like, BUT the way we got there changed regularly and often; going over it, under it and, indeed, through it.

In my opinion, whilst weaving is required, you cannot avoid the fact that open, honest conversations, where you *genuinely* mean people no harm, can never be replaced by any other strategy.

When have you learnt from your experiences?

- How often do you engage in open and honest conversation with staff?
- Why have you held such conversations?
- What do you do when your staff encounter personal challenges that impact upon their role in school?
- What unexpected ways around a challenge have you successfully navigated?

PART THREE

WHAT IS PURE COACHING?

PURE coaching empowers people to bring their best self to work.

Introducing Leadership Edge

At Leadership Edge, we seek to live by our strapline, mission and vision statements, and our values.

Strapline:

Empowering schools to create a holistic coaching culture.

Leadership Edge mission statement:

Supporting staff to feel empowered to bring their best self to school.

Leadership Edge vision statement:

It's time for a new model of coaching in schools, one that values both people and results. People want their work to have purpose and meaning; to be partnered in their on-going learning with leaders who provide a confidential thinking space for them to be truly listened to, where strengths are developed, and people are supported to create their own solutions to challenges.

Leadership Edge values:

Trust: We build relationships one by one; we keep confidentialities, we are non-judgemental (we haven't walked in your shoes). Your coaching session is PUREly your own agenda.

Credibility: As associates, we know about education and are accredited coaches; we all have educational roles.

Integrity: Serving our clients through a consistent and uncompromising adherence to strong moral and ethical principles. We enter coaching conversations with the intention of deeply understanding.

So WHY was Leadership Edge established?

Quite simply, I couldn't find another coaching company that provided the type of coach training for school leaders that I was looking for. As my frustrations with the quality of school-centred coach training grew, taking action became a matter of now or never. The now came in 2018.

> *'When you want something, the universe conspires*
> *in helping you to achieve it.'*
> **Paulo Coelho: The Alchemist**

From gaining my coaching qualification in 2005 until 2010, when the National College of School Leadership published a paper on coaching in schools, coaching was not part of educational leadership.

The following decade has seen an emergence in the popularity of coaching in schools and many leaders have the word 'coaching' in their job descriptions. Surprisingly, some 15+ years on, we still have no regulated coaching system.

Anyone can call themselves a coach... and many do!

I was aware that training for school coaches varied from a half day, to maybe two days of training, with no follow-up and no supervision.

I continue to find many teachers/leaders who find it a challenge to differentiate between coaching, mentoring, challenge and support, and professional dialogue.

'If I have coaching, does this mean I am failing?'

The other concern which was, and still is, often voiced is: 'If I have coaching, does this mean I am failing?' Some have watched colleagues being coached to improve their pedagogy. At Leadership Edge, we would call this support 'directive coaching', or the better-known term, 'mentoring'.

For us at Leadership Edge, we believe the exact opposite: your coaching experience will enable you to take the next step forward in your professional or personal life, whatever that is to you.

To develop coaching there needs to be a structure to build on

Using the East Park Academy journey as a model, we crafted what is now known as the Leadership Edge three-tier process to enable schools to create and sustainably build their own non-directive coaching culture.

What we do at Leadership Edge isn't rocket science.

We don't claim to own the secrets to great coaching.

In fact, it is part of our mission to help you understand how simple and easy coaching can really be.

Here are the key pillars of PURE coaching:

1. Knowing the difference between mentoring and coaching. Both are important in professional development; they complement each other. Ying and Yang. But if you smudge them into one big circle of greyness, the magic is lost. At Leadership Edge, we describe mentoring as the passing on of professional knowledge and being directive, and coaching as holding a thinking space – empowering people to reach the right decisions and actions for themselves.

2. Deep and broad listening. In normal life, 80% of our conversations involve listening to respond. In coaching, we listen to REALLY understand all layers of what is being said, and being left unsaid. This takes skill and practice.

3. Deep and broad questioning. Certainly, there is a range of 'question types', but being conscious of WHY you're asking them is key. How does this question benefit the person in this moment on their path to moving towards their goal?

4. Using a structure to shape the conversation helps to create a fulfilling experience. You've given time to each element of the thought process so the actions at the end have the best chance of being successful.

Yes, we know about neuroscience, leadership styles, values, limiting beliefs, habit systems, mindfulness, action setting... but those things will only have practical impact if the understanding and power of them comes from a readiness in the coachees themselves, at a time that is immediately relevant. That's why the four pillars have such power: they empower others.

When we create our own
thoughts, we own them
and look after them.

19.

Why PURE Coaching is Crucial for Well-being and Retention

I have seen the word 'coaching' emerge in educational and school policy documents, on job descriptions, and coaching itself being offered out as training courses. Coaching globally remains an unregulated skill set.

Increasingly, coaching in schools is used to improve pedagogy and move staff forward in their professional performance. What continues to perturb me is the wide variance in what constitutes professional coaching practice, the supervision of this and the future learning around the subject. Coaching skills, like all skills, should be ongoing, as new learning and thinking emerges.

At Leadership Edge, we share the benefits of a non-directive coaching approach through our testimonials, reflecting well-being and empowerment. We know that it remains rare for leaders to take time in the business/busyness of schools to enable themselves or their staff to regularly have the opportunity to reflect and create their own way forward. To many, it is *mission impossible!*

For successful leaders coaching is a no-brainer:
explore your thinking first and then act!

Against this background is the FACT that many early career teachers are choosing to leave the profession because they feel overwhelmed due to a poor work-life balance, and disempowered through a lack of control in their workplace impacting on their personal life.

The millennial generation that will be entering the school workforce in the immediate years ahead do not want this. It is the responsibility of our current generation of school leaders to empower staff to bring their best selves to work; to partner with their learning to enable them to serve our children to the best of their ability for the ever-changing future ahead of them.

For coaching to be of value there must be recognition that it is SKILLS-based and requires practice. The Leadership Edge model provides both coaching practice and supervision.

What we know from more than 150 coaching conversations that have followed the Leadership Edge three-tier coaching programmes is that the difference having a coach can make is humbling. The impact on personal well-being and gaining a feeling of empowerment and control are just two of the many benefits we share later on in this section.

Often in schools, the role and purpose of coaching is understood as being: 'The passing on of professional skills and knowledge from a person more experienced and/or knowledgeable in the subject'. This is frequently to correct poor performance or an intervention prior to competency.

At Leadership Edge, we call this strategy 'directional coaching' or 'mentoring'. Our aim is for coaching to be seen as an essential part of school life; an entitlement for leaders and teachers to have the opportunity to safely reflect upon their professional roles, or outside challenges which may impact on these.

There are ranges of different coaching models, which align to various points across the coaching spectrum. 'Instructional coaching' is a model that aligns towards the mentoring side of the coaching spectrum. This sometimes involves the use of technology to record practice and then a

It's time for a new model
of coaching in schools –
one that values both
people and results.

conversation is held to discuss this. One danger, as we perceive it, is that this can be a dependency model: *'Tell me what I need to do to improve so that I am not seen as lacking in competence.'*

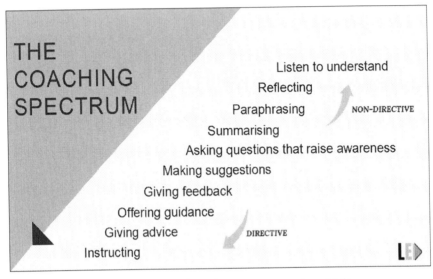

Figure 2: Leadership Edge endeavours to get coachees thinking in the non-directive range.

'A coach provides an opportunity to hold a "thinking space" for the coachee to think their challenges through, reflect upon their own thinking and identify a way forward that works for them.' – Jan Rudge

Everyone who starts on the Leadership Edge coaching journey begins at **Foundation Stage**. Here you will embed four essential coaching skills and experience being coached using the T-GROW model, one of the most popular and well-known coaching models.

Leadership Edge rose out of our passion for bringing future-focused coaching practices and working culture into schools. Our approach is designed to create a cascade effect, which will benefit the whole school, rather than the typical, expensive model of sending perhaps one staff member to train, with little effect on the rest of the school.

A cascade model of learning is cost-effective and sustainable.

Our three-tier accreditation system is based on what teachers and educators identify as the competences they look for in a school-based coach.

Assess.Coach

On our website, school leaders and staff can begin by taking our assess. coach five-minute quiz. This provides an overview of how they are currently feeling about aspects of their work and personal life. We call this process 'Bringing your best self to school', but the word 'school' can be substituted for any organisation or personal role.

On completion, you receive direct to your inbox a nine-page report. This is a great introduction to a first coaching conversation, or even the 'meet and greet, cup of coffee' session.

The report begins with a spider diagram overview and then unpicks further reflective questions from your responses. As you might expect, the reports vary considerably.

In example 1 below, I was curious about why the respondent felt they didn't expect to have low stress or a good values match. In example 2, why didn't this head teacher have clarity and purpose? All was revealed in the coaching conversation that followed!

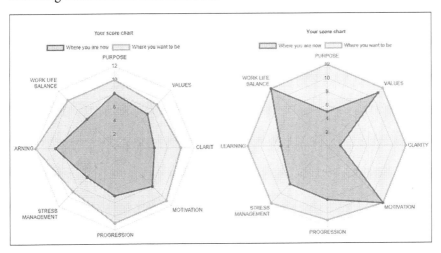

Examples 1 & 2: The front page of an assess.coach report for two leaders.

Should you coach early career teachers?

In 2019, I offered out assess.coach to my group of School Direct ITT students in mid-October, a few weeks into their training. I was curious as to what the responses of this group of student teachers would be just over a month in. I followed each quiz up with a conversation to unpick the outcomes. There was a huge variance in their reports (see examples 3 and 4)!

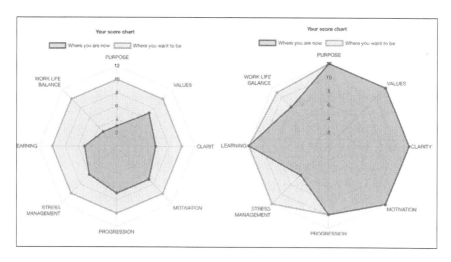

Examples 3 & 4: The front page of an assess.coach report for two trainee teachers, six weeks into their training.

In 2019, NQTs and RQTs were involved in coaching at East Park, another innovative move as in many schools, the leaders do not have a coach. An Outstanding Ofsted judgement is not the end of a journey for East Park Academy, but a milestone along the way. To remain outstanding is a team effort – the whole team!

Here are extracts from the thoughts of those staff on their coaching, in their own words.

Liz's story:

As an NQT, I have found coaching has really enabled me to progress and develop quicker, as well as to gain more confidence in myself and develop my thinking at a more rapid rate than I believe I would have without coaching.

Having a trusting and honest relationship with my coach has meant I have been able to be open and honest in all sessions as I knew I could talk without judgement.

Each week I would set a small goal towards reaching a desired outcome. In doing this and in turn reflecting on this, meant that each week I felt a sense of achievement. After a number of weeks of doing this, I began to feel empowered. This empowerment has come about as each coaching session has made me a stronger person, more confident and I know I have the power to make changes. It made me see I am in control of many aspects of my life and issues that I may face along the way.

Throughout coaching you find yourself letting go of leaning on or relying on others to find solutions for you, but replace this with the confidence to independently decide on what you want and how best to get there. The whole process makes you grow and become a stronger person who is more confident.

The empowering aspect of coaching allows you to overcome any concerns, worries, problems, difficult situations as well as reach desired goals. It gives you a strong sense of having control over these and seeing how you can influence your environment and outcomes.

For me coaching is about having conversations with my coach but at a deeper level than having conversations with myself. The conversation ripples go on long after the coaching session has finished and before the next coaching session has begun. Using the skills I have developed through coaching, I take a more critical approach towards my practice and my relationships with others.

Molly's RQT story:

Coaching is a self-care luxury that you should allow yourself to accept.

I learnt very quickly that coaching is not about a back and forth conversation and much more than an opportunity to just offload as I had originally thought.

By the end of the session, I felt like a weight had been lifted and I felt confident that what I had shared would remain confidential. I did not feel like I had been probed to reveal more than I wanted and was instead guided to delve further into the topic I had chosen to discuss.

I found myself thinking about our session long after it had finished, and the concerns I raised started to feel simplified and more manageable for me to overcome independently. I felt excited for our next session.

As a new teacher, I often feel like I have not yet earned the right to share my views/ideas; however, my coach has helped me see the value in my ideas and opinions.

If someone were to ask me about coaching, I would firstly pre-warn them that the experience will feel very strange to begin with and you might feel like pulling away. It goes against learnt human behaviour to share your experiences and talk to someone in a way you might write in a diary, completely indulgent and self-centred. However, if you give the experience a chance and allow yourself to trust in the process you will reap the benefits.

I would also say that you need to be brave when having coaching, especially at the beginning. It is easy to deflect from the real conversations you want to have through fear; however, **these conversations are the ones that need to be had.** I would also say, try not to leave a coaching session wishing you had spoken about something. If it's important and playing on your mind then it needs to be spoken about, otherwise you'll continue to carry the weight of that concern with you all week.

Most importantly, even in the most hectic and stressful of times it is important that you try to maintain your coaching sessions, as often you may feel like talking is the last thing you want to do, but it is often exactly what you need.

Jo's story:

I feel that my coaching journey has enabled me to be continually reflective of my practice.

I feel that the way in which I approach problems and challenges in my working life has changed a great deal. Coaching has allowed me a safe space in which I can discuss my concerns, my strengths, my weaknesses and my experiences, and realise the ways in which all of these aspects of my practice can shape and evolve the teacher I am, and help me to move forward towards becoming the teacher I want to be.

Knowing that there was someone within school who would listen without judgement, and not having concerns about the confidentiality of our conversations, allowed me to be more confident in my teaching and in my decision-making as I knew there would be a safe place, with someone I trusted in, where I could discuss the outcomes of these decisions and their implications moving forward.

I am more able now to think of ways in which I can continue to improve and use my self-reflection to develop my practice and effectiveness within the classroom.

I feel that I am a more decisive teacher within the classroom, and I know that my students benefit from my growing confidence.

By encouraging me to come to my own conclusions, I began to believe more in my own judgements and convictions and became more confident as a classroom leader because of this. Knowing that I was capable of generating these solutions was an empowering experience and without the coaching process I do not feel that I would have gained that confidence that quickly.

The benefits of coaching do not lie in someone else prescribing you with a course of action and outlining what you should do in order to overcome your challenges, but rather enable you to reach those decisions by making your own choices, setting your own goals and creating your own plan in order to move towards them. The process is one of empowerment and independence and encourages you to see that the answers that you are searching for are already within you and just require an open and safe space in which to lay them out, order them in a coherent way and map out the best way forward in order to achieve the goal that you have set.

What really stood out to me was that ideas were my own. I wasn't 'directed' but able to come up with the solutions to what had initially been concerning; through my coach's guidance I have been able to resolve my own issues, which made me feel good, in control and empowered.

Cascading coaching skills and practices

Leadership Edge aims to cascade coaching skills and practices throughout schools in a collaborative and organic way, at an affordable cost.

The major accrediting coaching associations seem unable to tailor their business models to accommodate the needs of schools. While their definitions of coaching and competence are useful, they do not take into account the particular challenges facing school leaders and teachers in applying coaching in an educational setting. Individual courses are expensive and time-consuming.

We have created and tested a set of individual competences at three levels: Master Coach, Practitioner Coach and Foundation Level Coach. These can be cascaded throughout a school by accredited in-school practitioners.

The momentum of PURE coaching can build quickly and effectively throughout a school.

20.

The Three-Tier System

Creating a coaching culture – the what and the how

There is a challenge in the school workplace. Instructional coaching (a directive coaching model) is used to raise attainment. Leadership Edge's vision is to provide a non-directive model of coaching, one that values both people and results. We refer to our model as **PURE** coaching.

Leadership Edge coaching sessions are purely the agenda of the coachee.

To break this into an acronym, as this book cover shows, the key elements would be that Leadership Edge coaching sessions are:

P – Personal

U – Unconditional – your own agenda!

R – Reflective

E – Empowering

Here we share the three tiers of our coaching programme, interspersed with direct quotes from participants along the way.

But first, how was the Leadership Edge associate team formed?

P – Personal

U – Unconditional – your own agenda!

R – Reflective

E – Empowering

Creating the Leadership Edge associate team

In 2018, with the East Park journey well underway and results now speaking for themselves, other schools and leaders were becoming curious as to how this progress was enabled.

With the support of my own coach and Leadership Edge co-founder, Hugh Todd, and with the knowledge, passion and skills of a small team of school colleagues, who were equally frustrated with the reputation of coaching in schools and committed to the value of establishing a non-directive, sustainable coaching culture, Leadership Edge was established.

These hand-picked leaders were invited to become associates alongside Hayley and myself. The criteria were that all associates had personal experience of leading in a school context.

All Leadership Edge Associates have or have had a senior leadership role in a school.

Those we chose without a formal coaching qualification from a recognised body would first undergo our own three-tier accreditation programme, which had emerged from the East Park journey.

Leadership Edge firmly believe that coaching is a deeply empowering pedagogy, which can benefit school leaders, staff and students alike; a significant shift away from a top-down, command-and-control direction, which is long overdue.

Leadership Edge is determined to challenge the many factors that work to prevent such a shift – attitudes, policy, budgets, time, training and more. We aim to help schools to build a coaching culture where not only is it 'the way we do things around here' but 'that's the way we are, we don't even need to think about it'.

'I thought that it was really clever how my coach managed to get me to answer my own questions and solve my own problems. She never told me the answer. She always made me think that little harder about

the challenges that I had and identify a clear way ahead. Coaching is empowering!'

The Leadership Edge three-tier accreditation programme for schools is a **cascade coaching** system that starts with the **Foundation Level**. The journey continues into **Practitioner Level** and finally **Master Level.**

For coaching to be of value, there must be recognition that it is SKILLS-based and requires practice. The Leadership Edge model provides both coaching practice and supervision.

At **Foundation Stage,** participants embed four essential coaching skills and experience being coached using the coaching model, GROW:

G – Clarify the GOAL

R – What is the REALITY of the situation?

O – What OPTIONS do you have?

W – Finding a WAY FORWARD

'The discussions I have had with my coach have questioned my way of thinking and allowed me to become more proactive, enabling me to provide myself with answers of how I can achieve my goals. I feel like I have got a challenging year ahead of me, but I feel much more prepared for it than if I hadn't had the coaching sessions.'

Foundation Coach Level

Participants learn about four coaching skills and practices; they receive a skills booklet and accreditation e-portfolio. Coachees will first meet (at times virtually) with their coach to begin getting to know each other. We call this our 'cup of coffee' session. They will then experience coaching as the coachee over four sessions, coached by a Leadership Edge Practitioner or Master Coach. Each coaching session is non-directive, PUREly their own agenda.

'During the first "cup of coffee" session we had to establish a change in working relationship from mentor to coach – I remember the coachee saying to me, "I'm looking forward to getting the answers from you"

and me explaining that as a coach, my role was to get the answers from him!'

The Foundation Stage e-portfolio is completed as the coachee develops their learning through each coaching session. Once coaching sessions are completed, the coachee then responds in writing to three reflective questions in which they summarise their understanding of the coaching process they have experienced. Their Leadership Edge coach provides a testimonial of their coachee's journey.

When this is complete, a final coachee conversation is held with a Leadership Edge Assessor who will ensure that the coachee can articulate their reflections on the Foundation Stage and identify their next coaching step. Once the assessor confirms that the participant is able to articulate clearly the process they have been through, they will be recognised as a Leadership Edge Foundation Coach.

'At the end of my session today I gained a real clarity on working out a clear pathway to something I have been very cloudy about for a very long time. A sense of purpose is beginning to return and my lack of motivation is disappearing.'

Practitioner Coach Level

Participants will have gained a Leadership Edge Foundation Coach accreditation and will continue to develop their knowledge of coaching skills and practices. They will receive a skills pack with four more advanced coaching skills and an e-accreditation portfolio.

They are required to coach two people for a minimum of six sessions, with at least one person being from within their organisation. A Leadership Edge Associate Coach will provide ongoing coaching for the trainee Practitioner Coach and supervision during this stage.

The new trainee Practitioner Coach will start with their own coachees by holding a 'cup of coffee' meeting so that they can get to know one another, and the coach can set the boundaries for each session ahead. THIS IS A BIG JUMP for the new Practitioner trainee.

What are the concerns?

How will I remember what to do?

How will I keep to time?

What if I can't think of a question to ask?

Limiting self-belief: I will not be as good as my own coach!

As the progression is made to Practitioner Coach, the supervising coach is there to dispel concerns and to talk through the coachee's challenges as they move into the coach role. The coachee wants to feel they can trust their supervising coach, that their confidentialities will be kept, that the coach will be non-judgemental and will listen deeply to them. Your Leadership Edge supervisor/coach is there for you throughout your Practitioner Stage journey.

'At our "cup of coffee" meet-up, he talked about his family which I immediately thought showed a level of early trust. I too felt the same and was able to warm to him with ease. I am delighted and quietly proud that I have been able to form positive and genuine relationships with each of the coachees that I have worked with.' LE Coach

Making the move to being in the coach seat yourself requires a SHIFT.

The flow of the sessions is now in your hands. This requires deeper reflection on what you learnt by being in the coachee seat and from the role model of your own Leadership Edge coach.

'You want to be able to fix things for your coachee and that is when you have to give the monkey back. It is not our problem as the coach to fix things for our coachee. Our job is to empower them to fix things for themselves by exploring options and providing a safe, confidential listening space.'

The Practitioner accreditation e-portfolio will evidence reflective feedback from both coach and coachee on the sessions led as coach and on the personal journey progressed through at this stage.

'The biggest reflection for me as the coach was that (he) said how beneficial he had found the coaching sessions because apart from his family, I was the only other person he had spoken to about these things. Coaching is not about looking back but moving forward and can become

the connection for people to explore some of these deeply embedded feelings in a proactive way to emerge stronger, to feel more confident and empowered by seeing their experiences through a different lens.'

At the start of each tier of coach training, the accreditation process is clarified. Everyone is equally assessed (standards) and it's a level playing field (accountability). A question often asked is, 'Does everyone become accredited?' No! There have been participants who have not met the standards; they get feedback and the option to address their gaps and redo the coachee conversation.

One of the most challenging aspects in the transition from Foundation to Practitioner Coach is that of holding back and holding silence.

'Stay curious a little longer.'
Michael Bungay-Stanier

In the words of three newly accredited Practitioner Coaches:

* ✱ *'I had to hold the silence today. My coachee replied, "You want to probe this further, don't you?" I said, "Do you feel you need to?" to which he continued to tell me about the situation that had arisen.'*

* ✱ *'As a coach, holding silence has become a more natural and comfortable part of the process because (a) I have been on the other side of the silence and I have come to appreciate that it is far from a negative phenomenon, but rather it is a purposeful and necessary part of the coaching session; and (b) as a coach during the silences, I can take the opportunity to consider how I personally might respond to the current line of questioning and the possible responses that a coachee might make.'*

* ✱ *'When I have been able to hold an awkward silence, I have seen the benefits of how it has helped my coachee succeed.'*

As Leadership Edge assessors, nothing gives us greater pleasure than holding the final coach conversation and sharing the ongoing journeys of our newly accredited coaches. The same goes when a coachee says to us:

'It feels great to be truly listened to – I feel valued!'

We all need to feel heard, whatever stage of our development and life we are at.

That is why every Leadership Edge Associate in the team also has a coach ☺

Master Coach Level

Participants will have gained a Leadership Edge Practitioner Coach accreditation and will receive the Master Coach accreditation e-portfolio, along with a log-in to the Master Coach area on our website.

The Master Coach journey is about looking beyond our school environment to see what learning we can be inspired by, taken from other work and businesses. Master Coach is a mix of personal development and new personal learning and reflection, addressing the: *So what next?* question.

There are seven stages to progress through at Master Coach level, starting with further self-awareness reflections over a consecutive period of weeks, using the model from the head of coaching at Google, David Peterson:

- What new thing did I do today?
- What worked well?
- What did I do?
- What one thing might I do differently tomorrow?

At Master Coach level, participants will be building a coaching culture within their organisation. They will coach three people in their organisation, and will have six coach supervision sessions with a Leadership Edge Associate.

The Master Coach accreditation e-portfolio requires a coach to provide reflective feedback on their coaching across their three coachees, together with reflections on their new learning. Models of coaching, books about coaching/leadership, neuroscience and research are all component parts of the Master Coach journey.

Often in schools, the role and purpose of coaching is understood as being: 'the passing on of professional skills and knowledge from a person more experienced and/or knowledgeable in the subject'. This can be to correct poor performance or as an intervention prior to competency.

Three newly accredited Master Coaches share their stories.

Louisa's story:

As a leader I have really changed my daily practice in this area, and it is becoming more and more natural to push conversations in this way – constantly empowering others, and at times showing my own vulnerabilities because, as Patrick Lencioni argues in *The Five Dysfunctions of a Team*, if we share our vulnerabilities in a genuine way, and not staged, then this can generate an increase in trust and confidence.

I was working with our business manager. I do not have a vast knowledge of her daily, weekly or termly tasks but her coaching issue in her first session was that she was feeling overwhelmed and was having trouble prioritising. As we worked through the Covey Time Management matrix it became clear to her that some of her time was not spent on the most important or urgent tasks she had to do, leaving her feeling 'behind'.

When reflecting on some of the changes I have made, I feel that I have accepted that being an achiever and a learner is part of who I am and that they are positive attributes which I need to embrace.

I now feel that I am ready to take this learning to a new role and I am looking forward to spreading the message of coaching wherever I go. Completing this programme has given me a stronger understanding of the kind of leader I want to be.

As a school we had been through a process called 'coaching'. The directive coaching model we had completed had left staff feeling vulnerable and negative, as it was NOT what staff now refer to as coaching. When I initially broached the subject of a PURE coaching model, staff were still wary.

> *Our Good OFSTED inspection I genuinely feel was due in part to our coaching model and staff feeling empowered to look for self-improvement.*

Staff who were initially reluctant to be involved in coaching have more recently been championing the process, and I can truly say that we have become a school where coaching is an integral part of what we do.

Coaching will allow a staff team to improve and look for solutions where possible. I have found that coaching empowers staff members, so that they feel trusted to move forward in their own area of practice.

> *I have my monkey image on the inside of my coaching file to remind me that it is 'not my monkey', and I don't have to take on other people's problems.*

Fast forward to the end of that academic year and we had all teachers completely on board and celebrating the benefits of our coaching model. Because of positive feedback and conversations, all staff members began to ask if/when they could be involved. This academic year we have a coaching model which includes all teachers, teaching assistants and office staff.

Cierán's story:

Stopping and taking the time to reflect is a crucial insight into the progress I have made. I am using coaching subconsciously, daily in my interactions with different people. Each relationship is unique and progresses in unexpected ways; to be proactive is vital.

An effective series of habits is forming, based on positive, compassionate, PURE coaching. My own self-belief and confidence are increasing, aided by my experiences and successes.

Coaching is an essential leadership tool to nurture trust in others and establish true culture. The test of a culture is how groups respond to sudden events and challenges.

I really enjoyed stripping away all of the elements I found important to live by, culminating in the top five qualities that I valued above the rest. It was no surprise, therefore, to realise how closely they aligned with my strengths. Looking for common connections in different ways of coaching; personalising it, adapting it and making it your own.

Merely having an obligation to change for a perceived sense of duty, rather than wanting to change because of a personal vision, desire or dream, seems counterproductive to me, and not in line with the PURE idea of coaching that I have attempted to advocate in my own experience.

Leading coach and author, Boyatziz, writes that great coaching could simply be 'like having a relaxed conversation with a close friend'. This I can relate to during my time as a coach: establishing an environment of safety, trust and respect, with no judgement and getting to the point in a relationship where deep and meaningful discussion can take place.

Any coaching discussion should always relate to the coachee's vision of a holistic, comprehensive expression of their 'ideal' self and future, including their dreams, passion, purpose and core values.

Judith Glaser in her book, *Conversational Intelligence*, talks about the need for a firm level of trust, so that new ideas and approaches can be tackled without fear of judgement. As she proposes, questions of discovery can be asked without a pre-thought answer, listening to connect to a person's aspirations, and they open the way for deeper connections.

Reflection is a special commodity, but one that can be neglected without priority and attention. It is easy to be in the moment, make progress but not spend the time to actually reflect on it afterwards. Completing the accreditation process has given me an excellent opportunity to take the time and truly think about the power of coaching, and the effects it has had on my own development, those of my peers and the school overall.

Completing my Master Coach portfolio has enabled me to do research and learn about coaching beyond education.

True culture in an organisation is everything: in order to achieve it people need to understand, respect, trust and communicate with each other. I am lucky enough to believe we have this in place.

With coaching in a school, there is no 'one size fits all' approach; each setting is unique and will need to forge their own path, tailoring and adapting their own model on their own respective coaching journeys. It will also need to take prominence on School Development Plans, and external stakeholders such as the governing body will need to be regularly informed. My own journey to become a Master Coach has been one of personal exploration and discovery, as well as deepening my understanding of those around me.

Rachael's story:

There is a challenge I continue to work on: I have to stop myself sometimes from talking about a similar situation that I have been in, to show empathy towards my coachee. I am aware that this is an area of development for me and I am very conscious of ensuring that each coaching session is time for my coachee to think and talk. I have my own coaching session for this time!

Reading articles or extracts about being an effective listener is an important part in reminding me of one of the purposes of coaching. I must remember that I am not there to solve problems for the person but only to hold a thinking space to enable them to come to a conclusion for themselves; to empower them to make decisions for themselves.

After reading Gallup's research article, many of the points highlighted resonate with me. In particular, some of the best leaders make the best coaches; is this because coaches are trained to provide time for their coachees to think and solve problems or overcome difficulties themselves? Or is it because they communicate more openly with people? Or that they model level 3 listening? Or all of the points?

There could be a number of reasons but having a coaching culture within a school certainly brings out the best in employees and provides them with the openness to talk to their employer.

After taking my assess.coach quiz for the second time, I know that I have come a long way to being where I am today.

I have grown a lot as a teacher and leader and enjoyed learning from great leaders at school. My job and work matter to me and I am passionate about everything I do.

I want to let others experience this and feel value themselves in knowing that they have it in them to seek the answers. There is nothing more powerful than overcoming something of difficulty by yourself!

I have thoroughly enjoyed working towards my Master Coach accreditation and have learnt so much from the research I have read. This has spurred me on to read more about the coaching culture of schools and look at how I could possibly get more involved with this. PURE coaching has really changed my outlook on life and filled me with the positivity and self-drive to believe that I am able to overcome so much myself; it's about spending the time on ME in order to make decisions. I want this opportunity for many others, so that they too feel valued and empowered.

Vision and mission

At Leadership Edge our aim is for coaching to be seen as an essential part of school life, an entitlement for staff at all stages of professional growth to have the opportunity to safely reflect upon their professional role, or any outside challenges which may impact on this.

We believe that people have the answers to challenges within themselves. Coaching provides an opportunity to hold a 'thinking space' for the coachee to think through their challenges, reflect upon their own thinking and identify a way forward that works for them.

Our three-tier accreditation system is based on what teachers and educators identify as the competences they look for in a school-based coach.

If we are to retain great staff in our schools, where we invest in each other for the benefit of our children/students, then this approach to partnering through giving staff a safe space to think for themselves MUST surely be an essential step in retaining committed staff members.

The top-down 'leader knows best' approach is not satisfying the needs of MANY staff in our schools right now. School staff (and beyond) value working for a leader who listens, who learns and who reflects themselves, and therefore knows how important this thinking space is for their staff; where a key leadership role is to grow the next generation of self-emergent leaders.

The benefits of having engaged and productive staff far outweigh the small amount of regular time a coaching conversation takes.

As the model matures in schools, coaching can then further develop to be across a family of schools in a MAT. We are currently now on this journey. As one early adopter of this shared with us:

'There is something very powerful in being able to confide in someone that you don't know and who doesn't work at your school. After two sessions I felt like I could completely trust my coach and the promise of confidentiality was very important because I could really open up and discuss my genuine worries and troubles.'

Our Leadership Edge journey continues. We are happy to have a conversation with you and explore how coaching can work for you, if our mission resonates with your thinking.

21.

The Added Value
of Non-Directive
Coaching

Becoming your best self

Prior to starting any coaching relationship, we suggest that a new coachee takes our assess.coach quiz. This provides the coachee with a copy of their responses, which are often thought-provoking and can create a great starting conversation with their coach.

There is nothing more powerful and humbling than to hear a coachee speak about the personal benefits of PURE coaching.

Here, I share (in their own words, and with permission) quotes taken from **Foundation Level** accreditation reflections.

But first, let me take you back to an earlier comment:

What we do at Leadership Edge is not rocket science!

Our role is to value and be non-judgemental about the journey individuals have travelled to date, and support them to construct a proactive way forward.

In the words of Susan Fowler in her book, *Master Your Motivation:*

> **'People always have motivation. The question is what type of motivation do you have?'**

Below are the words and feelings expressed by coachees. Maybe they will resonate with you as you understand more of why, at Leadership Edge, we consider our PURE coaching model a way forward to enable staff to feel more in control of their choices and actions. Notice how their remarks demonstrate how the coach helped encourage choice, deepen connection, and build competence.

The impact of PURE coaching on motivation, mental health and well-being

* 'When using the coaching space, I feel a weight being lifted.'

* 'Recently I have been feeling vulnerable and this may have been because of the changes (lockdown). However, since coaching I have felt a lot stronger.'

* 'I have taken the knowledge that simple, yet effective, questioning can help improve my mental well-being. I have also learnt that sharing the problems I may have will only help me turn those problems into solutions. My coach helped me see the wisdom of being more proactive in my role and reaching out for what I want, rather than sitting on the fence and waiting for it. Coaching has given me confidence and raised my self-esteem as well as improved my mental space.'

* 'I felt nervous and a little bit uneasy because I knew that I was talking about a topic that was difficult for me to discuss so openly.

I worried about getting upset. My coach was patient and kind and made me see that the problem I had been worrying about all these years really wasn't my problem. I turned an extremely negative thought inside my head to a positive one and this made me see things in a completely different way. I was incredibly grateful.'

* *'I then felt that negativity was a big barrier to me changing for the better, and the effective questioning my coach gave me helped me realise this and start to unpick how to really distance myself from these untrue beliefs about my teaching.'*

* *'It felt great to be listened to – I felt valued! I began to recognise what was within and outside of my control. Talking aloud helped me process my thoughts. The use of paraphrasing also helped me to listen to myself! My coach was really helpful guiding me through my thought processes and allowing me to change my mindset, to be more proactive.'*

* *'I viewed myself in a terribly negative way. I didn't realise that I am stronger than I ever gave myself credit for. My coach helped me to see that. He asked me questions such as:*

» *What do you want to gain from these sessions?*

» *Where would you like to see yourself in 12 months from now?*

» *How can you make sure that you get there?*

» *What obstacles could be in your way? What can you do about those?*

» *What advice would you give to someone else in your situation?*

» *What strategies can you put in place to support you if that happens?'*

* *I have experienced many difficult and wonderful times during my time as a teacher. Some of the more negative experiences have made me doubt myself and my ability to the point where I almost left altogether. I have come to realise that I am excellent* at what I do, and no other human has the right to make anyone feel inadequate.'

* 'Coaching for me is a safe thinking space. I can start to make sense of the millions of thoughts that go through my mind on a daily basis. By focussing in on the thought that has taken up the most brain space, the time with a coach allows you to reset, recharge and refocus thoughts into actions.'

* 'My second session was quite a deep session. We discussed many things and it was massively helpful, to not only be listened to, but to have someone understand in a non-judgemental way. The session enabled me to reflect on my own practice and my own career. This I found incredibly powerful, as we don't always have time to consider ourselves.'

* 'My coach has helped me think through situations and not simply "solve the loudest" at any point in time. This has in turn impacted on my capacity as a leader as it helps me focus on being more proactive and a little less reactive.'

From the coaches' testimonials:

* 'She was extremely honest from session one and told me about some of the situations she had faced and how these had affected her. By giving her the space to articulate these feelings, it was clear that these situations had caused her a lot of anxiety. By reframing some of her negative thoughts, she was able to navigate her way through some of these situations and see them in a different light, a more positive light, which empowered her to believe in herself.'

* 'I felt that he had been content to blame some of his issues on other people around him rather than reflecting on how he could have changed the outcome or influenced decisions, and this had become a reason for inaction for him. Leaving the session with a goal to inform the next session enabled him to take ownership of the action.'

* *'When my coachee began talking, it was clear that what she had gone through elicited a highly emotional response from her as a result of her values being dishonoured. She talked about kindness but how other people's behaviour had led her to question her own abilities. Her limiting beliefs applied to people who she had previously worked with and we were able to challenge whether the opinions of other people had been based on fact or opinion.'*

* *'During the session, it was so interesting to see how powerful it was to reframe her thoughts. There was a "lightbulb" moment and she said she had never thought about her situations in terms of strength before, and this shift was a way of breaking the pattern she had been a part of.'*

* *'Deep-rooted anxiety had affected my coachee personally. By discussing this during coaching, we were able to turn these negative experiences into ones where she could see them in a more positive light – she had the strength to walk away, not because she was told, but because she made the decision she would no longer want to work for someone who made her feel that way. The reframing of that negative thought allowed her to have a much more positive outlook. She was proactive in seeking further professional help around the issue (counselling) so that she could really get to the root of her feelings. This coupled with the coaching has allowed her to stop and reflect on the successes she has had.'*

With mental health and well-being higher on the national agenda than ever following the pandemic of 2020, we must recognise that benefits ripple out into not only improved school lives but improved personal lives too, and with a proactive and empowered attitude, you can indeed then:

Bring your best self to work.

Our team at Leadership Edge are on a journey of self-discovery, both as individuals and as a company. That's why we all have at least one coach. We practise what we preach.

22.

We Learn Through Stories

You're probably aware by now that I am a huge Ken Blanchard fan and have been for more than 20 years. He often shares leadership messages through telling a parable – a story that contains a message. As a primary school teacher, storytelling resonates with me and I continue to love sharing other people's journeys through their own learning pathway. That is why I feel that having the opportunity at each coaching level to articulate your own learning is powerful.

This book shares stories and experiences from people at the start of their professional journeys, from those in the midst of the action and others of us whose careers have taken us in a new direction following their deeply held passions and values. I have shared mine and Hayley's story and some responses from participants on our Foundation and Master Coach tiers. Here I share more of our coaching stories.

Primary head teacher Jo shares:

Coaching is a brilliant way to develop both personally and professionally. It improves performance and can enhance skills or help you to acquire new ones. Coaching has helped me to improve my productivity along with my teams. It has helped me to improve communication both formally and informally.

> *Coaching has helped me to have clarity, to prioritise and achieve my goals, which in turn has decreased my level of stress!*

It is purposeful and challenging. It is thought-provoking and helps you find solutions, develop and grow. Coaching is empowering. I think that one of the most profound aspects of coaching is about being totally honest with yourself – developing greater self-awareness. It is energising.

I would say that it has enabled me to set targets and goals more effectively and has improved my overall performance during the term. For me, coaching has provided me with greater autonomy and space to problem-solve. It has helped me to clarify the key goals for school for the coming year and to proactively set about achieving them.

Director of Education in a MAT Carl shares:

I would strongly recommend anyone to get involved in a coaching relationship. I have personally benefitted from coaching and would like to share that benefit by becoming a coach myself. I have introduced coaching approaches to working with colleagues. I have found it useful in my line-management conversations, but it has been especially powerful when working with those I do not have 'official' line-management responsibility for or hierarchical authority over.

There are many aspects of our current education system that I am not entirely satisfied with and I have found coaching is helpful in redirecting my frustration into some more constructive thinking and actions. I have also used coaching myself to find ways to engage others in deeper thinking around some of the areas that I find troubling.

Primary head teacher Juli shares:

One of the most important parts of the process, for me, has been to keep the staff informed. I have taken every opportunity to share my enthusiasm for coaching with them and begin to help them to think that there are other ways of providing in-school support – away from a carrot-and-stick model, which just puts people on their knees and doesn't really help them to 'buy into it'. It has been offered as a 'take it if you want it' or 'we're ready when you are' model, rather than a 'it's being done to you regardless' option.

Coaching helps people to connect.

Coaching has helped me to focus on a single aspect of school improvement and then work on it, rather than a more superficial scattergun approach, as there is always so much to achieve. PURE coaching has taught me to think – really think. I find that I revert back to TGROW to help me order and organise my concerns and then plan a way through, providing me with greater autonomy and space to problem solve. It has helped me to clarify the key goals for school for the coming year and to proactively set about achieving them.

I think that one of the most profound aspects of coaching is about being totally honest with yourself – developing greater self-awareness. It is energising. It gives you intrinsic ownership and, as a result, greater responsibility for your actions. It does not provide answers, but rather enables you to identify blocks/causes and reasons for inaction or underperformance, and helps you to articulate potential ways of remapping a way forward. Coaching is empowering, humbling and is in such contrast to other methods of school support I have experienced.

Secondary deputy head teacher Imran shares:

I can confess, I often want a lot done and normally yesterday!

Coaching allowed me to reflect starkly on how I am asking for the impossible, which creates frustration for colleagues and myself.

Moving forward, reflecting more and considering the most important points has helped me lead with more impact.

I was apprehensive of the coaching process at first; when anything is new there is always an element of apprehension. It was powerful to have a highly skilled coach and I have learnt a lot through this process. My coach did not make me feel as if I 'should have known…'. The PURE coaching process enables you to have head space to think through and clarify decisions you have reached.

My school role is to support leaders and the standards/teaching and learning agenda that go with being in Ofsted Requires Improvement category. My coach Catherine's skills guiding me through the sessions was powerful. I questioned why I'd felt apprehensive at first!

I have never been with someone who had no agenda. ☺ It was the most powerful thing being with someone with no context or baggage. Much depends on how open you as a coachee are prepared to be. It really is a space where you feel safe. What you are willing to bring is what you get out of the session.

Routes into coaching

Not everyone comes to coaching of their own volition. Not everyone we work with wants to follow the three-tier programme. That's why we offer a range of coaching services. A series of one-to-one coaching sessions is one of our offers and this was the option Kerrie chose.

Synchronicity comes in many different ways. I met Kerrie at the Schools and Academies Show. It has been my privilege to be her coach since visiting the amazing Stone Soup Alternative Provision Academy in January 2020. As she shares, there have been mutual benefits. Here is her story.

Kerrie, Principal, Stone Soup Academy – Alternative Provision shares:

Coaching for me has been one of those things that I didn't think I needed before I began receiving it.

As a senior leader of many years I had created an impenetrable wall around myself as I dealt with issues in splendid isolation.

Not uncommon I imagine of many headteachers and principals.

This wall can become very high when working in Alternative Provision as you are having to defend yourself against perceptions of it and in many cases you do not have the same network of support that exists with mainstream schools, where MATs regularly meet, share and support their leaders.

For me, a meeting with my Chair of Governors suggested that, for my performance management, a good thing would be to engage the services of a leadership coach. We are an outstanding Alternative Provision with awards and accolades, so my first response was, well, why? Surely having a leadership coach suggests some sort of deficiency of leadership; a need; something you are doing wrong that needs to be fixed.

Strangely though, the experience for me has been eye-opening and the discourse and safe challenges have opened my mind to the benefits of coaching. It has given me access to a conduit who can share their wide knowledge and experiences of many educational establishments and a range of educationalists, in a non-judgemental and positive manner, shining a light in many areas and, within this process, allowing me to challenge myself.

Having started the process being a closed book, I am now open and willing to listen. For me, leadership coaching is not a destination or something to be ticked off a list but rather, it is a leadership journey that I will continue to travel whilst I lead any organisation.

PURE coaching can help you to steer through very challenging times.

A leader in need

Sometimes leaders find coaching at the exact time that they need it. Jo, a serving head, and I met at what was a very challenging professional time for her. She was new in post with some staff unhappy at her appointment, due to an internal candidate not being selected for the headship.

Jo shares:

Without my coach I would never be still in headship. Coaching is a life-saver! It gave me the opportunity to reflect, steer through very challenging times and to give myself much needed time to develop my thinking and thought processes.

Through my coaching sessions I improved my leadership practice, and the sessions also had a significant positive impact on my personal well-being. I developed my knowledge of how coaching benefits all staff and the 'how to' of developing a coaching culture and bringing new teams together.

23.

Looking Forward

The future of Leadership Edge is in the hands of our current and future leaders as they seek to navigate their way through the journey that lies in front of them.

Our current associate team have started the journey. We hope that what we have created will serve schools well: support great recruitment and retention; support the mental health and well-being of all staff and children; make our schools vibrant places with creative, empowered people. Places where great learning inspires people to bring their best selves to work. Is this not what our children need and deserve?

PURE coaching is there for any individual who wants to self-improve or move forward from the past into a future where they can be their best self.

It can be challenging and endeavouring to be a great leader. Our hope is that this book will steer you forward to your next step towards becoming that best self.

Non-directive, PURE coaching, as we call it, focusses your thinking and develops enhanced listening skills. It takes constant practice and constant learning.

Teacher Standards require us to fulfil wider professional responsibilities and to demonstrate consistently high standards of conduct professionally and personally. Where do you turn when you need to offload or share frustrations? Friends, family, partner? Unsurprisingly, the responses of close family and friends can be emotionally driven. The difference with having a professional coach is that they are able to stay detached from the emotion and focus on moving your thinking forward; they have no agenda other than to serve your need and be at your side through the thinking process.

PART FOUR

MY
LEADERSHIP
LIBRARY OF
INSPIRATION:

20 books that have guided
my leadership journey

Leaders need to be learners too;
we stand on the shoulders of giants!

My top 20 'go to' sources for personal learning and self-development

It's so hard to select just 20 examples – there are so many great sources to learn from. World-leading coach, Marshall Goldsmith, talks about us 'standing on the shoulders of giants'.

I present my learning in the order in which it came to me and then share with you the stories behind each one.

1. *Feel the Fear and Do It Anyway*, Susan Jeffers (Vermilion, revised edition 2007). Self-talk and articulation.

2. *Gung Ho!*, Ken Blanchard (William Morrow & Co., New York, 1997). The importance of empowering people in the workplace.

3. *Who Moved My Cheese?*, Spencer Johnson (Putmans, 1998). Dealing with change.

4. *The New Leaders*, Daniel Goleman, Richard Boyatziz (Little Brown Book Group, 2002). The importance of emotional intelligence.

5. *Managing by Values*, Ken Blanchard (Berrett-Koehler Publishers, 1996). Self-awareness: know your core values.

6. *FISH!*, Stephen Lundin, Harry Paul, John Christensen (Hodder & Stoughton, 2001). Organisational values.

7. *S.U.M.O.*, Paul McGee (Capstone 10th anniversary edition, 2015). Unexpected difficulties/bad decisions/betrayal of trust. And *Self-Confidence*, Paul McGee (Capstone, 10th anniversary edition, 2019). The four support roles we all need.

8. *Self Leadership and the One Minute Manager*, Ken Blanchard, Susan Fowler and Lawrence Hawkins (William Morrow & Co., New York, 1982). Discover the magic of no excuses.

9. *The 7 Habits of Highly Effective People*, Stephen R. Covey (Free press, 1989). Powerful lessons in personal change.

10. *Our Iceburg is Melting* (2006) and *That's Not How We Do It Here*, John Kotter (Macmillan, 2006). Changing and succeeding under any conditions.

11. ***Strengths Based Leadership***, Tom Rath, Barry Conchie (Gallup Press, 2007). Building the team.

12. ***The Five Dysfunctions of a Team***, Patrick Lencioni (John Wiley & Sons, 2002). Building a trust-based team.

13. ***Colourworks***: (www.thecolourworks.com/) Communicating to be heard. Using this learning in a coaching conversation.

14. ***The Advantage***, Patrick Lencioni (Jossey-Bass, 2012). Solving team-based challenges.

15. ***Stand Out***, Marcus Buckingham (Thomas Nelson, 2011). Assess your strengths, find your edge, win at work.

16. ***Conversational Intelligence***, Judith E. Glaser (Bibliomotion, 2013). Everything happens through conversation.

17. ***Master Your Motivation***, Susan Fowler (Berrett-Koehler, 2013). In the business of becoming happier and more productive.

18. ***Dare to Lead***, Brené Brown (Vermilion, 2018). Rumbling with vulnerability.

19. ***The Coaching Habit***, Michael Bungay-Stanier (Box of Crayons, 2016) Say less, ask more, change the way you lead forever and ***The Advice Trap***, Michael Bungay-Stanier (Page 2 Books, 2020). Be humble, stay curious and change the way you lead forever

20. ***Entrepreneurial Leadership***, Joel Peterson (HarperCollins Leadership, 2020). The art of launching new ventures, inspiring others and running stuff.

RECOMMENDATION 1:

Feel the Fear and Do It Anyway, Susan Jeffers

Books seem to have come to me when I needed the message contained within. This one came to me as a recommended read via someone who had heard about my personal circumstances but had never met me.

How I came to read it

'I was attending a summer school lecture when I shared with a previously unknown course attendee that I was worried about my sister who was going through a tough time. She replied, "You need to buy her this book. Let's skip this afternoon's lecture, go into town and find it!"'

I was the one going through the tough time. My sister duly went to purchase the book, as instructed by person previously unknown, and, unsurprisingly, it was in stock!

So why do I think this is such a great book?

There are several phrases/affirmations that I have carried with me since my first read of this book in 1998, the first being:

'Whatever happens I'll handle it!'

This was useful both in my professional life as a then head teacher and in my 'new' personal life as a single mum with two teenage children.

Susan Jeffers wrote of learning to live your life the way YOU want to live it, to move yourself from a position of pain to one of power, energy and love. My journey of self-discovery began and has never stopped!

In my professional life in a challenging school, I would repeat this affirmation when I knew I was facing a difficult conversation, or when a parent spoke to me aggressively.

In my personal life, I stopped seeing myself as a victim and saw this as a new chapter in my life.

I acknowledged the need to fill my life with a variety of 'whole life' activities (what Susan calls the whole life grid), and I proved to myself that when one aspect of my life changes, I still have purpose and I can focus on what I want.

Family	Friends	Work
Personal growth	BEST SELF	Relationship
Me time	Contribution	Hobby

The challenge is that school leadership can be all-consuming, leaving your grid looking more like the one below and squashing those aspects of life that matter most.

Family	Relationship	Friends
Personal growth	Work	Best self
Me time	Contribution	Hobby

RECOMMENDATION 2:

Gung Ho!, Ken Blanchard

Rarely has a book touched me in the way this one did. I read my first Ken Blanchard book, *High Five*, while on a skiing holiday in December 1998 – not my normal holiday read!

My story

What an end of term it had been. In fact, what a year it had been! In January 1998, I found myself as an unplanned singleton again (the challenge when one party makes a decision that the other party is then forced to accept!). Six weeks later, my beloved dad suddenly died of a heart attack. My mum was clinically depressed before this and Dad's death threw us into even greater turbulence.

Then in July, my best friend's husband died as a result of an abseiling fall.

I was a head teacher, a newly single mum with two teenagers, a bereaved daughter, a carer for my mum, and supporting a bereaved friend. It was a year to remember.

On the positive side, Ofsted came and we got Good with Outstanding for leadership!

So, the last day of term finished and we had limped our way to the end. As Santa roamed the school corridors, ringing his bell and delivering gifts to our children, I was in a permanent exclusion meeting for a Year 6 boy, with unions and the local authority in attendance. It was agreed that the break would do us all good and we would see what the New Year brought. My prediction was more chaos around this issue.

After the year we'd had, a family skiing holiday (including my bereaved friend and her three children) had been booked, departing 26th December.

As school was locked up, I headed to the local shopping centre to buy some light-hearted reading to take with me. I spotted a book endorsed by Stephen Covey, author of *The 7 Habits of Highly Effective*

People. He had written, 'Ignore this book at your peril!' The book was *High Five* and I purchased it. The author, Ken Blanchard, was then unknown to me.

Looking out on a snowy hillside in Andorra, I picked up the book and started reading. The subtitle of *High Five* is 'The Magic of Working Together'. Ken reminds us of his mantra: 'None of us are as smart as all of us'. I was hooked!

On return from holiday, I went back to the bookshop and purchased two more of Ken Blanchard's books: *Gung Ho!* and *Raving Fans!*.

So why do I think this is such a great book?

Gung Ho! became my 'go to' book. It set out the guideposts that I felt were essential, not just for leading a business but equally applicable to leading a school.

The key learnings

- The spirit of the squirrel: worthwhile work.
- The way of the beaver: in control of achieving the goal.
- The gift of the goose: cheering others on.
- The book is an instruction manual about how to get the best out of your people.
- They NEED TO KNOW their work has purpose and is worthwhile.
- They NEED to have a say in helping the company (school) to get the best outcomes for everyone.
- They NEED recognition and thanks for their contributions.
- They NEED to be listened to.

Our children/young people have the same needs – to be partnered in their learning.

The book states: 'Too many employees leave their hearts at the office door.' We cannot have staff like this in our schools and organisations.

RECOMMENDATION 3:

Who Moved My Cheese?/Out of the Maze, Dr Spencer Johnson

One thing jumped out at me as I saw *Who Moved my Cheese?* in a bookshop: the Foreword was by Ken Blanchard.

It's a small book, large print, pictures and simple text. You can read the whole thing in less than an hour.

My story

With my own life going through a period of change, again this book came to me at the right time. It was part of my journey that led me to a heightened awareness of coaching and the benefits of being future-focussed during the upheaval of going through change.

So why do I think this is such a great book?

As with Blanchard books, Dr Johnson writes his message in a simple parable. It's about four mice who live in a maze and look for cheese to nourish them and make them happy. Cheese is a metaphor for what you want to have in life: a good job, a loving relationship, money, health, peace of mind.

The maze is where you look for what you want; it takes you through a journey of anticipated change, adapting to change quickly, enjoying the change and being ready to change again.

Within the book are some little gems of wisdom such as, 'Noticing small changes early, helps you to adapt to bigger changes that are to come'. Also included are good coaching questions like, 'What would you do if you weren't afraid?'

The key learnings

- Change happens: move with the cheese.
- Anticipate change: get ready for the cheese to move.
- Monitor change: smell the cheese often so you know when it's getting old.

- Adapt to change quickly: the sooner you let go of old cheese, the sooner you can enjoy new cheese.

- Enjoy change: savour the adventure and enjoy the new cheese.

- Be ready to change again: move with the cheese.

This is a great first read for emerging leaders and indeed for older students, and can form a good text from which to discuss student leadership. We want both our staff and our students/children to learn to adapt to change and to learn strategies to deal with stressful situations and unexpected and unwanted changes. Some children (and staff) are amazingly resilient in challenging situations and can be the catalyst for positive change among their peers. We should not underestimate the value of listening, providing a confidential and non-judgemental coaching space for everyone in our school to access.

Junior coaches, trained and supervised, can really make their contribution in such spaces.

As Junior (age 10) said:

'In Year 4, I wasn't making good choices. Then it suddenly came to me; this was up to me to make changes. I applied and became a Junior coach because I think I can bring this message to others, so they don't make the same mistakes as I did then.'

Learning from those who have trodden the road before us provides a powerful reminder that we choose our actions and our attitudes. Never underestimate the potentially sensitive topics children and young people can deal with more effectively than adults can, whilst at the same time developing student leadership.

As a secondary head teacher found out:

'In KS4, 14 girls got pregnant. The following year we introduced peer mentoring and it went to zero!'

Adapting to change quickly was forced upon the world in 2020 with the Covid-19 pandemic. Many people surprised themselves with the adaptations they were able to make; for others it was a time of immense challenge.

Dr Johnson's book is a simple reminder that things don't remain the same and part of life's experiences is learning to adapt as the need arises; sometimes by choice but also by circumstance.

The sequel, *Out of the Maze*, continues the story, with a focus on overcoming whatever beliefs are holding you back.

RECOMMENDATION 4:

The New Leaders, Daniel Goleman and Richard Boyatziz

This book came to me through the ongoing post-coach-training development. The senior coach team would gather us together on a Saturday morning and share learning with the group. We would then discuss and debate the learning, deepening our own thinking.

My story

After the trauma of sudden change, the period of undertaking coaching training and beyond became a total joy! I found myself surrounded by positive, self-reflective and appreciative people. It provided not only personal growth, but a safe space to reflect with a coach upon both home and school life, and the added bonus was how much new learning I was being exposed to.

This book was a follow-on from Daniel Goleman's most well-known of books, *Emotional Intelligence*, and the learning from Goleman still continues to have purpose and meaning for me today.

So why do I think this is such a great book?

The book really made me think about leadership and my purpose and role as a head teacher. In his description of the six leadership styles, Goleman shares two dissonant styles, pacesetting and command, and four positive or resonant styles, coaching, affiliative, democratic and visionary. These six styles remain as relevant today as when the book was written, and I still share this learning when facilitating leadership sessions.

The key message with leadership styles, in Goleman's words, are that they should be treated like a set of golf clubs: depending on the situation, a certain style will be the best fit. When in Special Measures, pacesetting and command can be required in the short term. Most leaders have a default style – for me, it's coaching! The warning is that the dissonant styles can be damaging to staff mental health if used long term. The challenge as a leader is to navigate your way through the styles. Don't be afraid to experiment.

Importantly, never abandon the style that got you to your current position. As a leader, you don't have to reinvent yourself; always stay true to your authentic self.

The co-writer of this book is Richard Boyatziz, who continues to be a leader I follow and is a regular contributor at WBECS (The World Business and Executive Coaching Summit).

The key learnings

He writes in this book that the crux of leadership development is self-directed learning, and talks about 'the five discoveries':

- My Ideal Self: who do I want to be?

- My Real Self: who am I? What are my strengths and gaps?

- My Learning Agenda: how can I build on my strengths and reduce my gaps?

- Experimenting with and practising new behaviours, thoughts and feelings to the point of mastery.

- Developing supportive and trusting relationships that make change possible.

The book introduced me to the value of 360 reviews, of actively seeking out negative feedback alongside the positive and the importance of sustaining leadership change; especially the power of mental rehearsal that non-directive, PURE coaching enables. It's as relevant today as when it was first published. It shines a light on the need for collective awareness within a team of emotions, and the 'open loop' of emotions, underpinned by neurology:

> **'Emotionally intelligent leaders know how to manage their emotions so that they can keep their focus, thinking clearly under pressure.'**

Yes – still applicable almost 20 years on!

RECOMMENDATION 5:

Managing by Values, Ken Blanchard, Michael O'Connor

My story

In December 2004, I was fortunate to spend a week with The Ken Blanchard Company on the *Gung Ho!* train the trainer programme. I attended with my Network Learning Community co-facilitator/ head teacher, Tracy Ruddle. We were the first two educationalists to ever attend this training. Part of the joy for us both was spending time with leaders from other work environments, with the common purpose of all wanting to be the best leaders that we could be.

You can't feel aligned with *Gung Ho!* philosophy or *Servant Leadership*, for which Ken Blanchard is internationally renowned, without delving into values. Among the many Blanchard books I read (and still read) was this one.

So why do I think this is such a great book?

Revisiting this book came at an interesting time for me. I was working with a MAT as they were growing and entering a new phase of expansion, new team members had been appointed and there was a need to revisit the strapline, the mission statement, the vision statement and their values.

As the book says, this process is not a quick one; it is essential that it is slow and deliberate, enabling time for reflection on words agreed and an in-depth understanding of their meaning. It's a process that has been greatly enhanced by one-to-one coaching sessions between each leadership team session.

The MBV (Managing By Values) process comprises of three steps:

1. Clarifying our mission, purpose and values

2. Communicating our mission and values

3. Aligning our daily practices with our mission and values.

The key learnings

- 'Genuine success does not come from proclaiming our values, but from consistently putting them into daily actions.'

- 'Communication happens naturally when you make things safe. It is through feeling safe that trust develops within the team.'

- 'Walking our talk is an ongoing journey.'

This is underpinned by the real need for leaders to listen to what their people are saying. They need to gather ideas and data; to collect success stories to share; to listen and lead!

- The MBV process acknowledges that each person 'including me' will have a part to play.

- MBV takes a lot of collaborative effort, at all levels, in all areas.

- Implementing MBV through an organisation is a long-term process.

> **'It's easy to spot commitment when you see it and even easier when you don't.'**

The challenge for a school is HOW to live its values and keep them as the guiding light by which to make strategic decisions. Do most leaders even consider their values when making key decisions? I fear not.

The second challenge is that of the competing voices of key stakeholders, the CEO, other key leaders, governors and board members. If a leader finds themselves making a decision that is against their gut reaction and personal values, it is stress-inducing and harmful to their mental well-being. This is not a subject to be taken lightly and given scant regard.

The bigger the organisation, the greater is the need for leaders to ensure clarity of message, with training and development opportunities for all, not just for teachers and not just about stuff. Everyone needs to be on vision.

RECOMMENDATION 6:

FISH!, Stephen Lundin, Harry Paul and John Christensen
Boosting morale and improving results.

My story

This book and the importance of living your values, both personal and organisational, came through my *Gung Ho!* training. The book was a gift from a friend when I left headship and went on to lead an Education Action Zone.

When my son Paul was 16, he got a Saturday job in a well-known stationery store. It was a large organisation and he had to attend staff training, which took place after work on Saturdays. The company led staff training on the *FISH!* philosophy, but through the eyes of my 16-year-old, the message went slightly astray. Paul told how, following the training, the company had painted the staff area blue and put fish transfers on the wall!

The story

This takes place in the Pike Place fish market in Seattle, where an extraordinary group of traders on the fish stall set out to sell fish by entertaining customers.

Traders would throw fish to each other. One would shout out: 'One salmon flying to Minnesota!' The others would then repeat this in unison. The crowd would gather as they stopped to watch the entertainment and catch some of the energy that flowed between the fish traders... and they would buy fish!

The key learnings

- Choose your attitude: there is always a choice about the way you do your work, even if there is not a choice in the work itself.

- Play: the second ingredient of an energy-filled workplace. Don't get overly serious. Have fun when you can, in a respectful way.

- Make their day: do all you can to create great memories; find ways to serve your people.

- Be present: be vigilant; look for opportunities for action. Be 'all ears'. Keep the focus and don't allow yourself to be distracted.

There MUST be a purpose to training: it needs to add and reinforce the values of the organisation.

Back to Paul

What the trainers had failed to share, or participants had failed to understand, was that, in the example in *FISH!*, these were the values Pike Place fish market had chosen to live by. But each organisation needs to work out for themselves what matters most: their values and their interpretation of these as seen in actions.

Fast forward one week. After the store had closed, a group of the young lads were in the store at the back of the shop, playing cricket using a ball of string and a cardboard tube (both readily available). The manager swiftly rebuked their action and told them in no uncertain terms to stop.

'But we're putting our training into practice and playing!' came the reply.

So why do I think this is such a great book?

FISH! is a short, humorous but thought-provoking read, reminding us that, at times, we may need to change our attitude to enjoy our work more. The key learning for leaders in this little book is the importance of staff training for all. And the purpose of the training needs to be clear; it needs to be relevant to role. It needs to add value, knowledge and understanding to the job role. Without clarity of message, time and resources will have been wasted.

Training time must not be a bolt-on, but part of the strategic, long-term plan, ensuring alignment with the organisational strategic purpose.

How do you check that time spent on training has been worthwhile in enabling staff to gain greater understanding? If no one is interested in an ongoing conversation about the new learning, how does that show that staff time in attending is valued or will make a difference to them or the organisation in which they work?

RECOMMENDATION 7:

S.U.M.O. (Shut Up, Move On) and *Self-Confidence*, Paul McGee

Let's talk about the first book, *S.U.M.O.*

My story

As touched on briefly in Part 1, in 2000 during her years as a student, my 16-year-old daughter was working in a local shopping centre in the customer services department. She was able to attend staff training delivered by Paul McGee. She recognised the similarities of Paul's work/training with what I was seeking to do at my school (a ten-minute walk from the shopping centre).

'My mum does this sort of thing at her school,' she told Paul, 'you should speak to her.' She then proceeded to give Paul my name and phone number. Paul duly rang me and, next time he was training in the area, he came to school to visit.

We did indeed have a lot in common. I shared with him the PSHE work we were involved in, known as 'You Can Do It', the bedrock of the message we wanted our young people to take with them throughout their lives: to be confident, persistent, organised, to get along with others and be emotionally resilient.

Paul shared that he wanted to write a programme for children, which he subsequently did – SUMO 4 Schools. Prior to this, he'd published *S.U.M.O.*, and several other books such as *Self-Confidence* and *How to Succeed with People*. He became known in the education world (and beyond) as an engaging motivational speaker. I would often go into schools and see his SUMO postcard displayed.

So why do I think this is such a great book?

Paul's work is as relevant to me now as it was then. *S.U.M.O.* is an easy-read self-help book, with principles that can guide organisations to change for the better and enable people within them to achieve better results in life – and have fun in the process.

A brief overview: the seven Rs

- Reflection: get off auto-pilot and press pause. Be honest with yourself. Live with increased awareness, attention and appreciation.

- Recovery: the pace of change can be exhausting. Modern technology often sees our minds constantly stimulated. We need to take time out. Sleeping can become a challenge. Recovery time is needed.

- Responsibility: take personal responsibility for your own well-being and welfare – the cornerstone to achieving the life that you want.

- Resilience: how we deal with the ups and downs, the setbacks, challenges and disappointments, particularly when the going gets tough.

- Relationships: good relationships are not a matter of luck; they are a great source of joy (heightened in 2020 by the Covid-19 pandemic). They are the bedrock of our life.

- Resourcefulness: a reminder to focus on what is in your life and not on what isn't. The importance of where we choose to focus our attention.

- Reality: be practical. Tell it as it is.

Post-script:

I now have a beachball (see *S.U.M.O.* chapter 5). Sharing this learning makes for a great group activity. I have used it with leaders and with governors while they were preparing to write their School Improvement Plan, and with new leaders and student teachers. But getting a beachball with six different-coloured panels was a challenge!

Now let's look at *Self-Confidence*, another Paul McGee favourite!

I often share learnings from this book when I facilitate training for aspiring leaders.

The key learnings

- Everyone needs someone to fulfil each of these four roles in their lives: 'Who are yours?' I ask.

- The Cheerleader: the great encourager. They can help to influence your thinking. (Think PURE coaching here!)

- The Challenger: they challenge your motives, plans and dreams. They help you explore your thinking in more depth. (Think PURE coaching here!)

- The Confidante: the people you trust. They listen to you; they provide emotional support, not answers. (Think PURE coaching here!)

- The Coach: the coach won't just challenge your thinking but will help you to explore what you need to do to achieve your goals. They will help you look to your own inner resources and think through potential opportunities. (YES! PURE coaching!)

I feel very aligned with this book. A key outcome for many coaches is that they tell us, as a result of non-directive coaching, that they do feel more self-confident.

THUMBS UP!

RECOMMENDATION 8:

Self-Leadership and the One-Minute Manager, Ken Blanchard, Susan Fowler & Lawrence Hawkins

My story

Okay, so I am a raving fan of all things Blanchard (and will remain so!).

Having attended the five-day train the trainer for *Gung Ho!*, I then signed up to attend the two-day *Situational Leadership* training. The principles of SL11 are set out in this book. As always, the learning is found within a parable.

I invested in the A1 laminated poster of the SL11 model. I still use it in my Growing Heads training course. It's a go-to model and also features within the Leadership Edge Master Coach module.

'Empowerment is something someone gives to you. Self-leadership is what you do to make it work.'

So why do I think this is such a great book?

The book talks about 'elephant thinking', this being an assumed constraint that limits your experience. Not realising your own power could be your greatest assumed constraint.

SL11 begins with self-diagnosis – identifying your DEVELOPMENT level (D4 high competence to D1 low competence).

What then follows is getting what you need – your SUPPORT level (S4 low directive to S1 high directive).

'When your competence is low, you need direction, when your commitment is low, you need support.'

The book shares the wisdom that in order to be a self-leader, it is your responsibility to get the feedback, direction and support you need. (Hence the value we place at Leadership Edge on all our associates also having a non-directive coach!)

Self-leaders are proactive in getting what they need to succeed.

Post-script:

In June 2019, I went to London to join a Blanchard session where Susan Fowler was presenting both the SL11 programme and her own latest book, *Master Your Motivation*.

What a privilege to talk with her about both subjects on what was the day East Park Academy had the Ofsted call! I shared with Susan a little of the East Park journey and the role PURE coaching and SL11 had played in developing their leaders. She donated her new book to Hayley and wrote her a lovely comment in the front.

Two days later, Ofsted declared East Park to be Outstanding. I presented Hayley with the copy of Susan's book, *Master Your Motivation*. The reality was, she already had!

RECOMMENDATION 9:

The 7 Habits of Highly Effective People, Stephen R. Covey

In my opinion, this is not a book to open at page one and read to the end.

I tend to use it in chunks (or habits). I agree with the many people I have now shared this book with – you need to read, then stop and think about the impact of this on you. As one middle leader told me, 'I take it to bed and read it and find myself having fallen asleep with the page still open!'

There are also words in this book that were not familiar to me on a first read, 'paradigm' being one. This refers to the way we see the world and a paradigm shift, when new knowledge appears that makes you look at something with new insight.

My story

I had purchased this book. It was probably recommended by someone at sometime. In 2001, I had the privilege or luck to be part of a Fulbright Scholarship enabling school leaders to gain insight into educational life in another part of the world. My group was matched with a group of school leaders from Solana Beach, California.

I was due to be staying with the Deputy District Superintendent, but at the last minute this was swopped around and I stayed with a primary school principal, Julie. To say our schools were different was a slight understatement; mine was socially deprived, Julie's wealthy.

One day when I was on exchange, I got speaking to Marge Hobbs, who was my original host. She had also led the school Julie now led. In conversation, she told me she was an official Stephen Covey trainer. I was excited on two counts: I had the book and was keen to learn more, and I felt there was much wisdom in the *7 Habits* that would benefit our school leaders within the Networked Learning Community. With the grant we had for our NLC activities, we could afford to fund Marge's flight so she could come to England and train us all. This came to pass.

To this day, I have continued to facilitate the learning within the *7 Habits* to our future leaders in our First Steps programme. This year (2020), it was delivered online in book-club format.

So why do I think this is such a great book?

This is another go-to book for me, great to guide you through a personal or a work-based challenge. The steps are universal and they work!

The key learnings

- Clarify your values, understand the principles of effectiveness, and ensure that what you do prioritise doing will enable you to have the energy to keep on doing it.

- The *7 Habits*:

     1. Be proactive.
     2. Begin with the end in mind.
     3. Put first things first.
     4. Think win-win.
     5. Seek first to understand before being understood (PURE coaching principle!).
     6. Synergise.
     7. Sharpen the saw.

This book is great to guide you through a crisis or change, although it's not always an easy journey. However, there are so many schools I work with who use this language in their day-to-day interactions – even an NQT I was recently speaking with, a sure sign that it's become part of the culture.

RECOMMENDATION 10:

***Our Iceburg is Melting*, and *That's Not How We Do It Here!*,** John Kotter

Let's look at the first book, *Our Iceburg is Melting.*

My story

No story to this one. I saw *Our Iceburg is Melting* in a bookshop, read it and loved it. In 2016 the follow-up book was written, this time about meerkats not penguins.

So why do I think this is such a great book?

Our Iceburg is Melting is well presented and easy to read (less than an hour). As a teacher with a primary background, I loved the story, the illustrations and the clear layout.

All Kotter's work is about managing and leading through change; but changes differ in their importance and complexity (take the 2020 pandemic, for example!).

If you follow Kotter's eight steps as laid out in *Iceburg*, they provide a really useful roadmap to navigate your way through a change project on both a small and larger scale.

The key learnings

- The 8-Step Process of Successful Change
  1. Create a sense of urgency.
  2. Pull together the Guiding Team.
  3. Develop the Change Vision and Strategy.
  4. Communicate for understanding and buy-in.
  5. Empower others to act.
  6. Produce short-term wins.
  7. Don't let up.
  8. Create a new culture.

This is further developed in *That's Not How We Do It Here!*. This time Kotter digs deeper into collaboration and the ability of high-performing organisations to quickly adapt as circumstances change.

Successful schools and organisations constantly scan the horizon, keeping abreast of the possibility of impending change. One size doesn't fit all; the skill is in choosing what does.

Good leaders know what's approaching and plan accordingly to keep afloat. They are realistic about what will work for their workplace.

The key learnings

My favourite takeaway from this book was the four-grid model putting team structure, behaviours and events together. Makes for a great conversation!

L E A D E R S H I P	Innovative, adaptive and energetic BUT chaotic	Well run AND innovative, adaptive and energetic
	Doomed!	Well run BUT bureaucratic and unable to change quickly
	MANAGEMENT	

RECOMMENDATION 11:

Strengths Based Leadership, Tom Rath and Barry Conchie

My story

I had read previous books around this subject – Marcus Buckingham's *Now Discover Your Strengths* (2005), which was co-written with the Gallup founder of this work, Donald Clifton. This was followed by Tom Rath taking over the life work of his grandfather, Donald Clifton, with whom he co-wrote *How Full Is Your Bucket?*, published in 2004 following Clifton's death in 2003. *Strength Finder 2.0* (2007) followed.

At the age of 16, Rath was diagnosed with a rare genetic disorder that causes cancer cells to appear in various parts of the body. Since the time of the diagnosis, Rath has been researching and experimenting with various ways of slowing down growth of tumours in his kidneys, adrenal glands, pancreas and spine. In 2012, he took sabbatical from his full-time position in Gallup to focus on writing a new book titled,

Eat Move Sleep (another interesting read).

This is probably my top most recommended book. It is science-based and I often describe it as the nearest thing you can get to a psychic reading! There is a code in the back of the book to the Gallup online assessment which takes 30–40 minutes to complete. On completion, your top five strengths will be revealed.

So why do I think this is such a great book?

The 2020 Gallup research revealed that people who spend 20% of their day working to their top strength feel both engaged and productive.

It dispels the myth that we should always be seeking to get better at our areas of development. Neuro-scientific evidence suggests we should focus on the innate strengths that we excel in. A great team will be built on the combined strengths that they have, and therefore more people can do what they naturally enjoy and do well. We don't have to be good at everything, we just need people in our team who complement us. Therefore, recruitment is paramount, to seek the person with both a skills need and an organisational fit.

The history of the Gallup strength-based movement

The strength-based movement began in the 1960s and over a decade ago, Gallup unveiled the results of a landmark 30-year research project that ignited a global conversation on the topic of strengths. More than three million people have since taken Gallup's StrengthsFinder assessment.

In recent years, while continuing to learn more about strengths, Gallup scientists have also been poring over decades of data on the topic of leadership. They surveyed a million work teams, conducted more than 50,000 in-depth interviews with leaders, and even interviewed 20,000 followers around the world to ask exactly why they followed the most important leader in their life. In *Strengths Based Leadership*, bestselling author Tom Rath and renowned leadership consultant Barry Conchie reveal the results of this research and the science behind it.

The Gallup StrengthsFinder assessment will provide you with

specific strategies for leading with each of your top five talents. It will also enable you to plot the talents of your team based on the four domains of leadership talent: executer, influencer, relationship builder and strategist.

There are 34 themes of talent the research identified within one of these four domains. I have not met anyone who, having done the test, felt that the results did not form an accurate analysis of their traits. What results can guide a team to do is to form job descriptions to complement the natural strengths of team players, and individuals can recognise where their value lies within the team.

DO NOT PANIC if you don't have a top-five strength within each domain; the stronger you are in one area, the more you will contribute in a situation where this domain is needed the most.

RECOMMENDATION 12:

The Five Dysfunctions of a Team, Patrick Lencioni

My story

This book came to me when I was on my *Gung Ho!* training with the Ken Blanchard Company. Our lead trainer, Gary, had recently purchased the book himself and shared it with the group. I thought it sounded interesting and purchased it myself.

So why do I think this is such a great book?

At the time, I was working with eight schools leading the Education Action Zone. There was a good programme of staff development established, including one I called (and still call), Growing Heads. It was for emergent school leaders who were at deputy or assistant head level.

Having read the book, it seemed to me that it was hugely important to bring this model to the attention of these new leaders. To this day, I continue to use this model with new and serving school leaders. In my coaching work, much seems to be about trust and teamwork (or lack of it!).

I also purchased (what were in those days) paper copies of the team assessment. This has never failed to produce lively debate among a group of workshop participants.

The model illustrates the need for a hierarchy of actionable steps, which can be used to overcome challenges that often become the hurdles a team needs to jump to become functional.

In my experience of sharing this work, a lack of trust and most certainly a fear of conflict always resonate with leaders.

This is a really practical book and can provide a road map by which a team can openly share their feelings (if there is trust) and navigate their progress (if they will openly contribute and not be nodding dogs!).

In our results-focused school lives, psychological damage can be (and is) inadvertently done by a leader who does not start by building trust and a follower who is too scared to speak out.

The book is especially useful for teams whose members are not used to speaking out and where the focus is just to listen and obey the leader. Team members have a responsibility to respectfully challenge and put forward their viewpoints.

RECOMMENDATION 13:

Colourworks, colourworks.com

My story

It was during my time at NCSL that I found myself in a workshop led by Insights.com. NCSL had engaged this company to share with school leaders the importance of self-awareness and of understanding yourself and others. As a follower of the work of Daniel Goleman on emotional intelligence, this resonated with me.

So why do I think this is such a great product?

The company can produce a detailed report which expands a participant's self-awareness and, when shared, increases a team's awareness of similarities, differences and the importance of good communication between team members.

By using this model, a team member can identify where their personality and communication are a best fit. The first comment is, 'I'm a bit of everything', or 'It depends on my situation/challenge at the time'. The reality is we all have a default style!

Self-awareness can really be enhanced by using and reflecting on this model. In my coaching, when challenges around communication arise, I have been known to signpost coachees to this model, to aid their understanding of their own behaviour in order to understand the best way to respond to others.

Adding the following straplines can help a person to decide what their default colour is:

- Red: be brief, be bold, be gone!

- Blue: give me detail.

- Yellow: include me.

- Green: show me you care.

Successful organisations divide tasks according to team member traits and strengths. This is a great tool for recruitment (quick!) and helpful in enabling teams to understand their co-workers. The language leaders use is important. Without conscious thought, the wrong choice of words can be damaging. Colourworks provides a light-hearted way of depersonalising a message in a non-confrontational way. In my experience, this has an impact on people longer term, often re-emerging in conscious thinking as situations are encountered.

RECOMMENDATION 14:

The Advantage, Patrick Lencioni

My story

I had previously read several Patrick Lencioni books, starting with *The Five Dysfunctions of a Team* (Recommendation 12), with *The Ideal Team Player* being the other standout book for me. I have often turned to his website, www.tablegroup.com, for some really useful, free resources, and I tune in to his own podcasts. More recently, in the 2020–2021 series, he was the first speaker in the WBECS full summit, speaking about *The Advantage.*

I often listen to his books on audio but, at times (and this is one of them), go on to buy the hard copy too. This book is full of really useful, thought-provoking ideas and, as always with this author, simplicity is at the heart of his messages.

So why do I think this is such a great book?

I have a great poster I often use in both leadership workshops and coaching conversations. It relates to the work Patrick has done around organisational health. I first read about this in the *Harvard Business Review*, February 2016 and it makes such common sense.

It gives just four steps an organisation needs to take if it is to be healthy:

1. Create a cohesive leadership team.
2. Create clarity.
3. Communicate clarity.
4. Reinforce clarity.

The Advantage brings together Patrick's wisdom from all his work into one great read. If you haven't read any of his other books, you can start with this one. The difference with this book is that it is not a fable, unlike his other work, but is a practical guide. I especially like the checklist on organisational health at the end of the book.

My big takeaway is the concept of creating a playbook, where individuals and teams can capture responses to his six key questions a team should keep asking to create clarity.

- Why do we exist?
- How do we behave?
- What do we do?
- How will we succeed?
- What is most important right now?
- Who must do what?

There is a real need for leaders to constantly revisit clarity of their organisational vision. The regular five questions on forms that Hayley uses are specifically to 'take the temperature' on aspects of school life and to check in that there is consensus of understanding. Great leaders consistently survey governors, parents and children, together with staff.

What six questions might children and young people ask their teachers and leaders? Now there's a challenge!

RECOMMENDATION 15:

Stand Out, Marcus Buckingham

My story:

Marcus Buckingham was well known to me as the author of *Now Discover Your Strengths* (2005), which was co-written with the Gallup founder of this work, Donald Clifton.

Stand Out moves on from Marcus's former work to encompass more of an ongoing assessment that a team can link into, with the potential of this becoming more of a performance management system – replacing many of the outdated models that still exist in companies (and schools!). The possible uses of this are wide reaching, but at its simplest, the 15-minute assessment reveals a person's top two strengths to the team. And the book contains insights for each strength on:

- You at your most powerful
- How to describe yourself
- How to make an immediate impact
- How to take your performance to the next level
- What to watch out for
- How to win as a leader
- How to win as a manager
- How to manage yourself.

During the pandemic of 2020, this was offered out at no cost. At Leadership Edge, our Associate Coach team took advantage of this opportunity and we also shared the offer on The Monthly Coach for subscribers to take advantage of.

When I revisited this book during the pandemic, we had recently expanded our Associate team and created a new regional team of Associates across the country. It is not a quick process to become an Associate; the building of relationships is paramount and various stages were entered into by those people who are now part of our Associate team. As a company we wanted to be responsive and innovative. We each took *Stand Out* and then looked at the strengths profile across our team. Working in strengths-based sub-groups, each group sought to answer the question: 'What next for Leadership Edge?'

What resulted were conversational videos recorded between Associates, now on our YouTube channel and on the shared learning page on our main website www.leadershipedge.org.uk. We also developed new coaching offers designed to meet the New Normal needs of schools that we had been hearing about. That became our new offer to schools, which we now call 'Adaptive Practices'.

So why do I think this is such a great book?

I believe, as Marcus intended, that the possibilities of working in a strengths-based way expand further the Strength Finder role of people using their strengths in the workplace, and being happier and more productive as a result, while taking a deeper dive into greater self-awareness and contribution to the team.

My belief is also that without using *Stand Out* creatively, there may well have been unexplored opportunities. Using it properly has the added bonus of the team developing relationships further with like-minded colleagues that, without these sub-groups, may not have happened.

As with all tools and models, it's HOW you choose to use them that really makes the difference.

Why not use this model and put together like-minded colleagues to review policies or to become a working group on an organisational/ whole school issue?

In an educational setting, what about cross MAT teams observing, writing notes and feeding back to colleagues? I think the possibilities of working in this way might uncover new ways of moving forward that have been previously unexplored.

RECOMMENDATION 16:

Conversational Intelligence®, Judith Glaser

My story

I first came across Judith as a WBECS speaker. With so many excellent thought leaders presenting in the annual summit (which actually spans nine months), as a participant you need to be selective. But Judith's session was always a must for me. Into my third year of following her work, she was running a WBECS-linked course for coaches around her new book, *Conversational Intelligence*®, the result of studying neuroscience across the globe and making the science understandable to her followers.

It was another (expensive) training course but, again, as with coaching way back, I felt compelled to join and learn from this knowledgeable lady. The training began (all remotely, as Judith came from America), with WBECS members across the world participating.

Sometimes opportunities were time limited. The training began with monthly webinars, pre-reading and reflections to do in between. We began in May 2018. The course comprised of an introduction and then seven monthly sessions to take us through to December 2018.

It was in month six that Judith revealed in session that the brain tumour she had been battling for years had returned. Her story of how she used science and conversation, rather than chemotherapy and drugs, was incredibly thought-provoking. Her work with WBECS at no other time focused on her own situation and until that point, I was unaware of her medical history.

She explained that she was now intending to begin treatment, having hugely exceeded and defied the medical prognosis that by now she would not be alive. When you hear of people who walk their talk, there is no better example than Judith modelled.

She explained that she would continue with our sessions for as long as she could and asked for no more than our positive thoughts that she could see us through to the end of our course and pass on her knowledge. As a back-up, she recorded sessions seven and eight.

Session seven did take place, with Judith giving us all an update on her health; the session then proceeded to run as all others had. In November 2018, we received an emotive video message from Ben Croft, the CEO at WBECS, informing us that Judith had passed away. Session eight became a mixture of gratitude to Judith for her work, and a commitment that her work would live on, along with extracts from the pre-recorded session.

So why do I think this is such a great book?

With a diagram, known as Conversational Intelligence® Dashboard, Judith demonstrates the spectrum of what this means neurologically, in terms of the conversations we hold.

Neuroscience is opening up new understanding as to how our brains work. This has increased my understanding of the science behind trust. Trust lives in the Pre-frontal Cortex; distrust lives in the Primitive and Limbic Brain.

TRUST involves actively bringing the following behaviours into your interactions with others:

TRANSPARENCY – RELATIONSHIP – UNDERSTANDING – SHARED SUCCESS – TRUTH-TELLING

Judith advocates priming our conversations for trust by creating a healthy mental, emotional and conversational environment that activates higher levels of partnering. When trust exists, your conversations with others produce more openness, candour, courage and caring. Our PURE coaching model endorses this knowledge. Trust is when we believe others will deliver on their promises.

Judith shares other scientific facts: when we trust others, we experience higher levels of oxytocin, a neurotransmitter that creates higher levels of bonding and mutual success.

Judith advocates double-clicking the 'opening the deeper connections' that are linked deeply in others' minds. Asking, 'What does that mean to you?' or 'How do you envision next steps?' are very powerful questions to deepen your conversation.

By double-clicking, you can better understand how others see the world. You gain clarity and understanding of what triggers others, and also a deeper understanding of others' perspectives, their deeply held beliefs, and their unique points of view.

Judith talks about what she terms the 'Tell-sell-yell' syndrome, where leaders/people are addicted to being right. It is only at the transformational level (level 3 listening/conversation) that we co-create and co-regulate.

Further facts about neurotransmitters: for healthy conversation, we need oxytocin, dopamine and serotonin. This results in high trust where we can be partnered in our learning (eg by our coach) and be proactive. Unhealthy or fearful conversation is driven by cortisol and testosterone, which makes us resistant to progress as we seek to protect ourselves.

Organisations can become hugely political places, where distrust exists. This organisational mentality and the fear it can generate has the ability to destroy individuals and change initiatives.

As a great leader, the aim should be for the organisation to be non-political. BUT REMEMBER, however good you are as a leader there will always be someone who comes along to test you, or worse, to metaphorically 'stab you in the back'! This can destroy self-worth and make you doubt your ability to lead your organisation forward. In such times, taking space to build yourself back up to thinking rationally is crucial, leading to a greater understanding that this is potentially someone else's agenda in operation, and not necessarily any fault of your own.

At Leadership Edge, we believe that we best serve others by partnering (non-directive coaching), and not by being directive and telling.

In Judith words: 'Everything happens through conversation'.

RECOMMENDATION 17:

Dare to Lead, Brené Brown

My story

Another great listen and a recommendation from the *Blanchard LeaderChat Podcast*. I was inspired and immediately downloaded the book!

So why do I think this is such a great book?

Brené Brown describes her research study, looking at the future of leadership and the barriers and obstacles to what she describes as 'daring leadership'.

In the book, she outlines the four skills needed to become a courageous leader.

1. **Rumbling with Vulnerability.** A great phrase! Brené assumed that the biggest barrier to courageous leadership would be fear, but her research indicated that fear is not a barrier. Leaders she interviewed admitted to being fearful much of the time. The real barrier is how people prepare themselves to deal with the fear. She shares how it is critical to understand that we all self-protect when we feel scared, defensive or vulnerable. She describes the importance of curiosity when Rumbling with Vulnerability, staying open and asking questions. The book shares 16 different ways we can become a daring, courageous leader.

2. **Living into Your Values.** Leaders constantly must do tough things, give hard feedback, put bold ideas into motion while being unsure of the outcome, and take many risks. Courageous leaders are able to do this consistently because they operate with a clear set of values and behaviours. The book shares how to operationalise these so they become guiding principles.

3. **Braving Trust.** This can be tricky because many leaders don't know how to talk about trust. Direct reports have to trust their

leaders in order to have honest conversations, and both parties have to be in an unarmoured position. Highest performing teams are built on a foundation of trust. Building trust is a skill that can be taught and learned.

4. **Learning to Rise** covers the ability to reset after an error or mistake. The ability to be resilient helps leaders learn from mistakes quickly, share those learnings, and continue to move forward in a positive way. It is a skill that every leader can learn.

There is a useful free online leadership assessment tool that can be accessed at www.daretolead.brenebrown.com. Well worth a look!

RECOMMENDATION 18:

Master Your Motivation, Susan Fowler

My story

I had previously read *Self-Leadership* and *The One Minute Manager*, which Susan had co-written with Ken Blanchard. In summer 2019, the day Hayley was to hear that the inspectors were coming the next day, I was in a London workshop, hosted by the Blanchard Company and led by Susan Fowler.

I always tune in to the monthly *Blanchard LeaderChat* podcasts (highly recommended). Susan was the featured author in one of these, so I knew a little about her new book, which had just been published.

Susan was talking about 'Situational Leadership' (another great model for leaders to use) and shared a little of her new work with the group. I took the opportunity to buy a copy of the book at the event and, having received 'the phone call' from Hayley with the Ofsted news during the break, I shared with Susan a bit about Hayley's journey and how she was a leader who had most certainly 'mastered her motivation'. As mentioned earlier, Susan very kindly gave me a copy of her book to pass on to Hayley, and wrote her a lovely message inside.

Hayley, like myself, totally resonated with the message of this book. We have had many discussions around its value and use in education. It is a book that is used and recommended by both of us in our ongoing work around school leadership and PURE coaching.

Susan Fowler explains: Optimal Motivational Outlooks are the 'health food' of motivation, because they promote fulfilment of the psychological needs proven by science to be at the core of human thriving.

What are the forces behind your actions?

- It's a self-defining activity for me.

- It enables me to demonstrate important values.

- I derive a sense of meaning from it.

- Pure fun and enjoyment.

- The fulfilment of a deeply felt sense of purpose.

- A conscious and deliberate choice to do the right thing.

- Because of an almost automatic way of being.

- An unexplainable interest and attraction.

- I've always gravitated to it naturally.

These statements reflect three optimal Motivational Outlooks: Aligned, Integrated and Inherent.

Suboptimal Motivational Outlooks are the 'junk food' of motivation. A suboptimal Motivational Outlook means that the reason for your motivation is unlikely to provide the positive energy you need for accomplishing your task or goal. This is especially true if the task or goal is complex, complicated or requires sustained attention. Even routine tasks you hope to integrate into your life on a regular basis (such as flossing your teeth every night) will prove challenging with a suboptimal Motivational Outlook.

The three suboptimal Motivational Outlooks are Disinterested, External and Imposed. If you ever notice the reason you're pursuing a goal or doing a task is for one or more of the following reasons, it's time for a shift!

- Pressure – I have to do it (I fear what might happen if I don't).
- There's the promise of a tangible reward or incentive.
- I don't care.
- To avoid feelings of guilt, shame or disappointment that would come from not doing it.
- I don't have the energy to manage what's required.
- To avoid damaging a relationship with someone who has expectations of me.
- I am too overwhelmed.
- In the hope I will receive people's respect.
- An expectation that it will bring me power and/or status.

Shifting occurs when you consciously align your goal to relevant and meaningful values, connect to a noble sense of purpose or recognise the joy you experience when pursuing your goal or doing the task.

Reflect on your shift.

Notice if you find yourself popping into a suboptimal Motivational Outlook. Be mindful of what you experience physically and emotionally when you think about a goal or a task that opens up a spectrum of motivational possibilities for you to choose from. You can make the decision to choose an optimal Motivational Outlook over a suboptimal one.

So why do I think this is such a great book?

Often the challenges people are experiencing and bringing to coaching sessions revolve around one of the three scientific truths Susan explores: people need to create choice, connection and competence.

Prior to having Susan's book, I spoke of motivation as being intrinsic or extrinsic. I knew from my Brierley Hill days, when we had little money to incentivise people, that motivation needed to be intrinsic!

Susan opened my thinking up to reflect on this differently, using her own model of a spectrum of motivation (2013), from being suboptimal, disinterested at worst, to external motivation and imposed motivation, through to optimal motivation where it becomes inherent, aligned and integrated.

It is most certainly a practical model to unpick challenges around both yourself and a person who is presenting you with challenges.

RECOMMENDATION 19:

The Coaching Habit and *The Advice Trap*, Michael Bungay-Stanier
Let's start with the first book, *The Coaching Habit*.

My story

Since joining WBECS in 2015, Michael has been one of my 'must listen to' presenters. I like his style; he is not a typical or conventional presenter, but an open and honest coach, often with a quirky yet memorable way of sharing his thinking. (I'm thinking here of a webinar I joined early in lockdown 2020, when the session comprised of him making his favourite cocktail and relating this to his message.)

His book features in our Master Coach programme and is fast becoming a firm favourite with our participants. Often a worry new coaches have is how to ask good questions that will open up the thinking of their coachee. Within *The Coaching Habit*, Michael presents his seven guiding questions.

Michael's mantra, which he always returns to, is that, as coaches, we should: 'Stay curious a little longer'.

The subtitle of the book is, 'Say Less, Ask More and Change the Way You Lead Forever'. Michael's beliefs around this are what got him recognition as Canada's number one coach and one of WBECS most popular presenters.

As a coach, forming and practising good habits are a continual work in progress. A regular dose of MBS confirms and reinforces the importance of this.

So why do I think this is such a great book?

Michael begins his book by referring to Dan Goleman's work on emotional intelligence, where coaching is named as one of the four effective leadership styles. Despite it being shown in research from the *Harvard Business Review* that coaching has a 'markedly positive' impact on performance, climate (culture) and the bottom line (results), Dan Goleman writes that it is the least used of the six leadership styles he identifies.

Scant coaching training that is predominantly theoretical, no supervision or follow-up learning and no time figuring out how to translate these insights into action (by having a coach to guide you through this), all contribute to failures in deploying coaching effectively.

From the start at Leadership Edge, we have differentiated clearly between coaching for performance and coaching for development. Michael provides a great definition: coaching for performance is about addressing and fixing a specific problem or challenge; it's everyday stuff; it's important and necessary.

Coaching for development is about turning the focus from the issue to the person dealing with the issue. Michael states that this conversation is rarer and significantly more powerful. Coaching for development (or PURE coaching, as we at Leadership Edge call it) calls you forward to learn, improve and grow, rather than just getting something sorted out.

Michael simplifies his advice: 'A little less advice, a little more curiosity; find your own questions, find your own advice'.

He suggests the use of coaching questions as a great starting point:

- The kickstart question: What's on your mind?
- The awe question: And what else?

- The focus question: What's the real challenge for you?

- The foundation question: What do you want?

- The lazy question: How can I help?

- The strategic question: If you're saying yes to this, what are you saying no to?

- The learning question: What was most useful for you?

RECOMMENDATION 20:

Entrepreneurial Leadership, Joel Peterson

My story

Synchronicity appears once more. As a regular listener of the *Blanchard LeaderChat Podcast,* in March 2020, I heard Joel Peterson sharing about his recently published book. I enjoyed it so much, I listened to it several times and of course purchased the book.

At this time, I was mulling over the need I was increasingly feeling to put the Leadership Edge PURE coaching methodology into print. Add to this that my *Stand Out* assessment had revealed me to be a pioneer and creative as the top two strengths I can bring to a team, and that my Strength Finder profile identified my top two personal strengths as strategic and maximiser, it felt like the message and purpose of reading this book was to galvanise me into action.

As I delved further into the book, Peterson's 'four essential basecamps' resonated strongly with me:

- Establishing trust.

- Creating a sense of mission.

- Building a cohesive team.

- Executing and delivering results.

So why do I think this is such a great book?

All leaders are change agents; great leaders are intentional, staying true to their vision and agenda. Peterson likens this to a gardener who, by watering, weeding and protecting his plants from pest and disease, creates a nurturing environment. He cannot grow crops, only foster the environment in which plants thrive.

Linking in to the previous recommended read, he talks about building a brand one conversation at a time, an action at a time, a decision at a time, with the purpose of helping people engage and connect.

Peterson writes about the importance of a team's mission, values and strapline and the need for these to uniquely describe three things:

1.   What we do.

2.   How we do it.

3.   Who we are.

He writes that the behaviour and conduct of a leader is every bit as important as skills and expertise, and that culture is driven directly by the way leaders behave, how people treat each other and the stories told and retold, which become part of company lore and the kind of behaviour that is tolerated or not.

He also writes about securing a team, the selection process and onboarding of new team members. He highlights eight mistakes that companies can make in the process of hiring; well worth a read. His message is 'hire for values, consistency, an ability to work well with others and specific skills, in that order'.

Peterson writes that the best leaders see coaching as a natural part of their responsibilities in trying to make the company successful. (Coaching for performance or development, though?) He makes the point that every entrepreneurial leader should consider coaching a priority and writes that, 'This means finding joy in others' progress, celebrating it when it occurs and giving feedback when it falls short'.

The other noteworthy part of the book for me lies in what Peterson calls 'Map 5: How leaders can fall short in their communication'. He identifies three mistakes that often result in poor communication. The first mistake is quantity – they do not communicate enough; they assume information is flowing throughout their organisation when communication gaps can widen. The second is one-way communication and the third mistake is not communicating directly and honestly.

Entrepreneurial leaders interact with people. They have a mindset of participation and not control; they believe two-way openness builds trust. Peterson's belief is that communication is the meta skill of a great leader.

The curiosity for me is why some organisations, who are in challenging and complex difficulties, seem to have no problem with recruitment and retention, while others struggle, even those on a more even keel.

I would suggest that happy, well-motivated staff with optimal self-motivation are not working in a state of fear (refer back to recommended reads 17 and 18). A great leader consistently measures how people are feeling through conversation in different forums. This may be in passing, a scheduled meeting or via feedback from other leaders in the organisation.

Great leaders constantly reinforce the vision and values while key messages are given with clarity to staff. They set the expectation that we are all contributors to a common framework.

This is the reason why, when recruiting, great leaders take their time and do their homework first. With reference to Patrick Lencioni's work, they check that their potential new recruits are hungry, humble and smart. They get the right staff and then work to keep them optimally motivated. They are committed to the success of all individuals.

Peterson quotes the words of William Hutchinson Murray about the power of commitment. This really resonated with me as it was a quote I remember having on my noticeboard at Brierley Hill Primary:

'Until one is committed, there is hesitancy, the chance to draw back, always ineffectiveness. Concerning all acts of initiative (and creation) there is one elementary truth, the ignorance of which kills countless ideas and splendid plans; that moment one definitely commits oneself, and then providence moves too.'

I guess the time is always right to do what's right. So, the commitment to put our journey into print is made. This is shared with the team.

Now over to the universe. Here we go ☺

Conclusion

So, there you have it – a learning journey via 20 great books. Your own top 20 books will chart you through your own learning journey, so maybe you will want to do this yourself.

The purpose of a journey is to ultimately lead to a different place; only you can chart your course. A good destination is one you reach that brings you joy and happiness, and you collect these markers along the way. On such journeys, mistakes are made and you have to find a way to get back on track, but it can be done!

A key purpose at Leadership Edge is to support school leaders in creating a workplace where staff bring their best selves to school. This will not happen without the purpose and motivation being directly led by themselves.

At heart, I am a primary school teacher. I have two grandsons, both currently at primary school. I have a vested interest in wanting the boys to have a wonderful school experience, both at primary school and beyond. I don't want their teachers to be exhausted, stressed and overwhelmed by the pressures that can exist within a school. I need to say – so far, so good! They have loved every teacher they have had, so a big thank you to them!

Thinking back to Hayley's teacher, Mrs Smith, we need many more classes to be taught by such inspirational teachers, whose legacy reaches far beyond a school year.

To the two fantastic head teachers, the late Pete Welch and Coral Johnson, who have shaped and influenced my journey, thank you for investing and believing in me.

To the new school leaders who have gone on to lead in other schools, but who played their part in the Brierley Hill journey, thank you too.

As human beings we need to reach out and connect. I do not believe our purpose in life is to just deal with the stuff that comes our way. We need the ability to sift through the stuff and keep only those elements that enable us to live a life of purpose and happiness.

Can this be done in a school or in other organisations? YES, IT CAN.

Let us not underestimate the value of articulating our thoughts and feelings in a safe space where we can honestly think through, without other 'noise', what we want our school/work life and our personal life to be like, and then proactively move towards that goal.

At Leadership Edge we call that thinking space PURE Coaching.

I invite you now to take a look at my 12 top leadership tips. Maybe focus on one each month as you continue your own learning journey.

One offer to each reader: if you would like a conversation that relates to one of the questions Hayley and I have posed in Parts 1 or 2, we would be happy to offer you a complementary conversation about it.

To find out more or to share your story, please contact me at: jan@leadershipedge.org.uk

Jan's 12 top tips

In the course of facilitating leadership training, I consistently return to key messages I have gained and aligned with along my leadership pathway, and offer these out to groups. I know many of you, like me, collect words of wisdom and use them to inspire or motivate, remind or redirect at certain moments in time.

Here are my top 12 frames of reference.

1. Be true to yourself and your own values.

2. What matters most?

3. Someone at some time will let you down.

4. Do what you can, where you are, with what you've got.

5. Whatever happens, I'll handle it – Susan Jeffers.

6. People should not miss out on important times.

7. Spot the welfare of your staff; it is your duty of care.

8. Saying thank you means a lot.

9. Only apply for the school and role that feel right for you.

10. Grow hearts and minds; be kind and true to yourself.

11. A good leader is a learner. Who are you learning from?

12. Stay curious a little longer.

How to connect with us

@edgeschools

le_purecoaching

http://linkedin.com/in/catherine-hulme-69933466

jan@leadershipedge.org.uk

www.leadershipedge.org.uk
www.purecoaching.org

Other sources of support

As good as coaching can be, coaches are not and would not profess to be experts in the many subjects that may arise during a coaching session. A comprehensive table of other sources of support is downloadable from our book's website – purecoaching.org/resources Council websites/local authorities often have localised support for people to access, but this PDF is a starting point and shows some of the national organisations you can signpost people to.

A JOURNEY THROUGH THE EAST PARK DATA

Standards 2016 – 2019

	2016	2017	2018	2019
Reading	59% EXP 4% EXC	73% EXP 24% EXC	73% EXP 24%EXC	77% EXP 27% EXC
Writing	53% EXP 3% EXC	62% EXP 25% EXC	73% EXP 25%EXC	77% EXP 27% EXC
Number	55% EXP 1% EXC	70% EXP 25% EXC	74% EXP 27%EXC	77% EXP 27% EXC
GLD%	43%	61%	73%	77%
National GLD %	69%	71%	71.5%	71.8%

Yr1 Phonics	2016	2017	2018	2019
School	56%	68%	89%	92%
National	81%	81%	83%	82%

Yr2 retake phonics	2016	2017	2018	2019
School	72%	89%	95%	100%
National	91%	92%	92%	92%

KS1	2016	2017	2018	2019
Reading	44% EXP 11% GD Nat 74%EXP 24% GD	65% EXP 24% GD Nat 76%EXP 25% GD	80% EXP 28% GD Nat75% EXP 26% GD	84% EXP 27% GD
Writing	31% EXP 4% GD Nat 65% EXP 13% GD	64% EXP 12% GD Nat 68% EXP 16% GD	77% EXP 21% GD	80% EXP 24% GD
Maths	49% EXP 4% GD Nat 73% EXP 18% GD	70% EXP 22% GD Nat 75% EXP 21% GD	78% EXP 33% GD Nat 76% EXP 22% GD	84% EXP 30% GD

KS2	2016	2017	2018	2019	PROGRESS
Reading	48% EXP Nat 66% EXP 19% HS	54% EXP 14% HS Nat 72% EXP 25% HS	81%EXP 21%GD 105 Scaled NAT 75%EXP 28%HS 105 Scaled	84% EXP 33% GD	3.24 Well above average
Writing	75% EXP 4% GD Nat 74% EXP 15% GD	49% EXP 2% GD Nat 76% EXP 18% GD	87%EXP 13%GD NAT 78%EXP 20%GD	84% EXP 24% GD	2.63 Above average
SPAG	59% EXP 0% GD Nat 73% EXP 23% GD	67% EXP 20% HS Nat 77% EXP 31% HS	78%EXP 25%GD NAT 78%EXP	79% EXP 35% GD	
Maths	46% EXP 0% HS Nat 70% EXP 17% HS	66%EXP 11%HS Nat 75% EXP 23% HS	83%EXP 25GD 105 Scaled NAT 76%EXP 24%GD 104.4 Scaled	83% EXP 34% HS	3.60 Well above average
Combined R/W/M	35% EXP Nat 53%	36% EXP Nat 61% EXP	73%EXP 9% NAT64% EXP 10%HS	81% EXP 21% GD	

- Data didn't significantly move until 2018.
- All key assessment points are above national by 2018.
- Shift with higher-attaining pupils came between 2018 – 2019.

Acknowledgements

We are coaches. We know it's good to set a challenging goal and go beyond your comfort zone! We also know that having a team around you makes all the difference. As the book says in the early pages, people often play a part in a journey in sometimes unexpected, but much appreciated ways.

Jan: Thank you to Hayley, who found time to work on this book amid the challenges of 2020. It has been my privilege to work alongside this talented school leader. To Steve and my children, Gemma and Paul, for believing in this book and whom I constantly use as my sounding boards!

To my long-standing friend, Angela Chapman, for proofreading the script and who has so much more attention to detail than I do!

To close friends who have lived a big part of my story with me from Brierley Hill days onwards.

Hayley: Thank you to Jan, my consiglieri, who is with me at every step. To Tom, Eleanor and Jon for surviving life living with a head teacher. And to the incredible East Park staff who have stuck with me during the journey. You are and continue to be our inspiration!

From us both: To the Associate team at Leadership Edge for their encouragement, with a special shout out to Mike Wilkes, for spending hours reading the scripts and feeding back with his wisdom.

To Dan Smith who has illustrated this book – we love your pictures, Dan!

To Beth, for your wisdom and guidance through the process of our writing and publication. To Alexa and her team from The Book Refinery for getting this book published.

To everyone who has been significant in the lives of US BOTH, too numerous to mention – thank you all for the part you have played.

About the Authors

Jan (pictured on the left) is director of Leadership Partners; she is a qualified leadership coach, facilitator of the NPQ national leadership programmes and creator of her own leadership programmes, which fit alongside the national ones. She works across two multi-academy trusts. She also leads initial teacher training for a teaching school.

Her passion lies in empowering our future generation of school leaders to not just have the organisational skills of school leadership, but also to partner and listen to their staff, enabling them to feel empowered too, so our schools can be happy and productive places for both staff and children to work and learn in.

She is the founder and director of Leadership Edge, a company she set up in 2018 to support other schools to develop their own sustainable non-directive (PURE) coaching culture. She works alongside an amazing team of coaches, all with a school leadership background, together with Stephen who designs and manages all aspects of their websites and Dan who provides great illustrations.

Hayley (pictured on the right) is the head teacher of East Park Academy in Wolverhampton, a 720-place nursery and primary school. The school is part of Manor Multi-Academy Trust (MAT).

She supports heads across the MAT and beyond as an LLE, leading the continuous school improvement 'creating futures together' through her strategic leadership role.

Hayley is a founder member of Leadership Edge and has taken the Leadership Edge PURE coaching model, which was created at East Park, and engaged staff throughout the MAT in gaining coaching accreditation at all three tiers. She is a sought-after leadership coach.

The year 2020 has seen coaches working beyond their own schools to working across the MAT.

Hayley oversees the Manor MAT coaching programme, which currently involves 107 coaches and trainee coaches across six schools. Coaching has provided a lifeline for staff during this year's global pandemic.